Daughters of Grace

Other Books
by this AUTHOR:

~ *Connecting*

~ *Deborah and Barak*

~ *Esther: A Story of Courage*

To order, call 1-800-765-6955.

Visit us at www.reviewandherald.com
for information on other Review and Herald® products.

Daughters
of GRACE

Experiencing God
Through Their Stories

TRUDY J. MORGAN-COLE
Illustrations by ROBERT HUNT

REVIEW AND HERALD® PUBLISHING ASSOCIATION
Since 1861 | www.reviewandherald.com

Published by Review and Herald® Publishing Association, Hagerstown, MD 21741-1119

Review and Herald® titles may be purchased in bulk for educational, business, fund-raising, or sales promotional use. For information, please e-mail SpecialMarkets@reviewandherald.com.

The Review and Herald® Publishing Association publishes biblically-based materials for spiritual, physical, and mental growth and Christian discipleship.

The author assumes full responsibility for the accuracy of all facts and quotations as cited in this book.

This book was
Edited by Penny Estes Wheeler
Art direction by Patricia Wegh
Designed by Trent Truman
Illustrations by Robert Hunt © 2009 www.roberthuntstudio.com
Typeset: Berling 10/16

PRINTED IN U.S.A.

12 11 10 09 08   5 4 3 2 1

Library of Congress Cataloging-in-Publication Data

Morgan-Cole, Trudy, 1965-
    Daughters of grace : experiencing God through their stories / Trudy J. Morgan-Cole.
    p. cm.
    1. Women in the Bible—Biography. 2. Bible—Biography. 3. Christian life—Biblical teaching. I. Title.
    BS575.M578 2008
    220.9'2082—dc22
                                2008031879
ISBN 978-0-8280-2383-2

CONTENTS

FOREWORD

Sometime during my academic career as an English major, I came across the following quotation by Christopher Morley: "From now until the end of time no one else will ever see life with my eyes, and I mean to make the best of my chance."

As I've enjoyed the profiles of biblical women contained in this book, I've wanted to rewrite that quotation to say: "From now until the end of time no one else will ever read the Bible with my eyes, and I mean to make the best of my chance." That's what author Trudy Morgan-Cole is doing—making the best of her chance and sharing her best with us.

Trudy has won writing awards for her articles and stories, written top-selling books, and taught writing workshops. She is, without argument, a creative talent. And she is, above all, an insightful Christian writer.

Here she has put her talent to writing about the select women whose stories have been preserved in the Bible. There's a reason these women are in this timeless, sacred Book. Their experiences have meaning for us today. There are lessons to learn, examples to follow, pitfalls to avoid.

Trudy covers them all. Sometimes she suggests likely details about their lives, but always she remains true to the biblical text. These aren't fictional stories. They are profiles of real women much like us—sometimes too much like us. And each profile ends with hope—the same hope that God can use each of *us* and help our names go down in history.

I have had the privilege of editing these biblical profiles for *Women of Spirit*, the magazine that originally published them. Trudy's column "What a Woman!" is in its fourth year and continues to bless readers and help them find relevancy in their Bibles.

For indeed, these women—and the Bible as a whole—have something important to say to us.

—LORI PECKHAM, *Women of Spirit* editor

"The grass withers and the flowers fall, but the word of the Lord stands forever"
1 PETER 1:24, 25

EVE

"Curiosity killed the cat" we warn children—and perhaps cats!
But is it wrong for a grown woman to be curious? Is it OK to want to know more,
to explore, to push the boundaries? Eve would probably have some advice.

Her crime wasn't a great one. She didn't kill anyone, assault another person, destroy anyone's property. All she did was to eat a piece of fruit. She broke a simple rule. And though we don't know her motives for sure, the most likely motive is simply that she was curious. She wanted to know more—so she tried something she'd been told was off-limits.

From that simple choice, according to the Genesis story of human origins, a whole nightmare of sin and suffering spiraled out of control. A woman we know as Eve stood in a garden, next to a forbidden tree, listening to the tempting talk of a sentient snake. She was newly-created, full of wonder and fascination about the beautiful world she'd been placed in. She and her husband Adam had been made the rulers and caretakers of this world. And God had given them only one restriction: Don't eat fruit from the Tree of Knowledge of Good and Evil.

What an interesting label for God to place on the forbidden tree! Wouldn't a name like that just entice you to check it out? And isn't knowledge a good thing?

The words "good" and "evil" probably didn't have much meaning for Eve, the first woman. There was no evil in the perfect world God had given to her and Adam.

There was no evil lurking in her heart, either—just the desire to know and understand what was around her.

The story of the first woman's decision to disobey God—the Fall, as Christian theologians often call it—is a short scene at the beginning of the Bible. There's not a lot of detail or elaboration; after the serpent tells Eve that the tree will make her as wise as God, Genesis 3:6 simply says:

"When the woman saw that the fruit of the tree was good for food and pleasing to the eye, and also desirable for gaining wisdom, she took some and ate it. She also gave some to her husband, who was with her, and he ate it."

Some people have interpreted this story as saying that human curiosity, the desire to know and learn, is a bad thing, that God is punishing Eve and Adam for trying to know more, to become more, to change their situation. Was Eve's sin—the first sin—really curiosity? Is the message that we should simply accept our limitations and our lack of knowledge, and not try to push past our God-imposed barriers?

Though different cultures have different mythologies about the start of human existence and human problems, the idea of a curious woman causing problems is a common theme. The Greek myth of Pandora's box tells the story of a beautiful woman and her partner Epimethus–a sort of Greek Adam and Eve, who lived in a paradise-like world. Pandora had a magical box, or (in some versions) a jar, which she was told never to open. Pandora's curiosity got the better of her, and she peeked into the box. All the evils of the world flew out and got into the air, infecting humanity forever.

Pandora's story sounds like a mythologized version of Eve's: curious woman does what she's been told not to do, and all humanity suffers. Is it really so wrong to be curious, to want to learn and know more?

The Bible constantly tells us to seek wisdom, and praises both women and men for being wise. Proverbs 23:23 advises: "Buy the truth and do not sell it; get wisdom, discipline and understanding."

God created us with the desire to learn, know and grow. Human beings are always searching for more knowledge, exploring and experimenting. And that's not a bad thing. Eve's story reminds us, though, that our curiosity needs boundaries. We can't foresee the results of our quest for knowledge. God can, and so God places limits on what we can and should do with that knowledge.

It wasn't wrong for Eve to explore her beautiful garden home. It wasn't wrong for her to pick fruit from the trees and eat it. It wasn't even wrong for her to be curious. What was wrong was that she disobeyed God's one clear command, stepping outside the boundaries He had set for her. Ever since then, we humans have been stepping outside those boundaries, and paying the price.

I think of another woman, thousands of years after Eve. Her name was Marie Curie, and she was one of the first great woman scientists of the modern era. She discovered radiation. From her experiments in her Paris lab, discoveries have come that have changed human history. How many people have been saved from an early death by radiation treatments for cancer? And how many people have been killed by atomic bombs?

Can we blame Marie Curie for nuclear weapons? Of course not. She couldn't foresee all the results of her discoveries. She was driven by the urge to know and explore—just as Eve was when she went to look at the forbidden Tree of Knowledge. But scientists who develop bombs *are* responsible for stepping outside God's divine boundaries, which tell us to love our neighbor and to preserve life.

Can we blame Eve for all the troubles humanity has suffered? Perhaps rather than blaming a single woman for a single choice, we need to see Eve as a symbol of the curiosity we all experience. We all want to know more, to try new things, to go new places and push our boundaries. And that's not wrong! Without that kind of ambition and curiosity, no new discoveries would ever be made, nobody would solve problems or take up positions of leadership. What the world needs—what the church needs, what your community needs—is a curious woman who wants to discover new ways to do things, new solutions to problems.

Eve's story reminds us that our curiosity needs boundaries.

But what God asks of curious women—and men!—is that their desire to lean and grow and know be guided by the boundaries He has set. Most important among those boundaries are the two Great Commandments Jesus gave:

"Love the Lord your God with all your heart and with all your soul and with all your mind and with all your strength. . . . Love your neighbor as yourself" (Mark 12:30-31).

Keep those commandments as your guidelines to mark the boundaries—and set off on your own voyage of exploration and discovery with God's blessing.

SARAH

Have you ever felt like God is laughing at you?
Maybe you'll have the last laugh.

She'd only ever wanted one thing in her life, really, and that was a child. It was what she'd been raised to expect—that someday she would present her husband with the first in a line of sons who would carry on his name and his heritage. As if there wasn't enough pressure, her husband had received a message from the Lord telling him that his descendants would be as numerous as the stars in the sky (Genesis 15:5).

By the time Abraham got that message, Sarah was already beginning to worry. She had been married for several years without bearing a child. People were beginning to look at her with pity, to whisper the dreaded word "barren" when they thought she couldn't hear. Yet even after God's promise, years went by and still Sarah's womb remained empty. Being child-less was more than just a personal sorrow for Sarah. Her husband was an important man, wealthy by the standards of desert nomads, destined to be the chieftain of a great tribe. But without sons, even a wealthy man was powerless. Sarah's infertility threatened Abraham's standing in the eyes of those around him. It seemed like a personal rejection from God—the God who had promised Abraham a family, yet failed to bring a baby to Sarah's arms.

More years passed. Sarah grew old. She passed menopause. It was now obvious to everyone that she would never bear a child. God would have to find another way to fulfill His promise. Abraham seemed confident that God would come up with a solution, but in her heart, Sarah doubted.

Then one day strangers arrived at their tent. Sarah stayed inside, preparing some food to offer their guests, while Abraham talked with the men outside. Through the open tent flap she heard an amazing conversation.

"'Where is your wife Sarah?' they asked him. 'There, in the tent,' he said.

"Then the Lord said, 'I will surely return to you about this time next year, and Sarah your wife will have a son'" (Genesis 18:9, 10).

Sarah couldn't believe her ears. One of their mystery guests spoke with the power and authority of God Himself—and He was promising that she would have a baby within a year.

She looked down at her body—old, withered, weary. She couldn't imagine this tired old body springing to life, growing a baby inside, giving birth. It was the most ridiculous idea she'd ever heard. After all these years of unfulfilled promise, who was this stranger coming to her door and claiming to bring the promise to fruition? He had to be crazy. The Bible tells us what happened next:

"Sarah laughed to herself as she thought, 'After I am worn out and my master is old, will I now have this pleasure?'

"Then the Lord said to Abraham, 'Why did Sarah laugh and say, "Will I really have a child, now that I am old?" Is anything too hard for the Lord? I will return to you at the appointed time next year and Sarah will have a son.'

If we accept that we serve an all-powerful Creator God, we have to believe that nothing is too hard for Him.

"Sarah was afraid, so she lied and said, 'I did not laugh.' "But he said, 'Yes, you did laugh'" (Genesis 18:12-15).

Sarah heard God's plan for her, and she laughed. It was so outrageous as to be unbelievable. She just couldn't take it in.

Have you ever laughed at God's plan for your life? Most likely you've never had angelic messengers show up at your door and make predictions for your future. But God's plan for your life may be revealed through the words of Christian mentors—a pastor, teacher, or friend who says, "I could really see you in this role." God's will might be revealed through a need someone asks you to fill. Or perhaps His dream for you is hidden within your own deepest, unspoken dreams for yourself: "Someday I'd like to try . . ."

Those dreams often seem extravagant, impossible, out of our reach. We'd like to serve God, to do His will for our lives, but fulfilling His plan involves resources we haven't got, skills we know we lack. Like old, tired Sarah we look at ourselves in the mirror, hold up our unimpressive selves against the shining brilliance of what we could be—and we laugh. It's impossible. It's unrealistic. God's dreams are too big for us.

God confronted Sarah head-on with the fact of her laughter. "Is anything too hard for the Lord?" He asked. Of course the answer is no. Sarah would have had to admit that if God wanted a 90-year-old woman to have a baby, He could certainly do it. It was no more amazing, after all, than creating the entire universe at His command. If God could create life, than He could bring life to an old woman's womb. If we accept that we serve an all-powerful Creator God, we have to believe that nothing is too hard for Him.

Most of us can accept that idea in principle, but it gets a little harder when we apply it to ourselves. If you'd asked Sarah, "Do you believe God can do anything?" I'm sure she would have said, "Yes!" But if you said, "Do you believe that you, Sarah, are going to have a baby within a year?" —well, that would be a different story. So ridiculous, all she could do is to laugh.

If you were asked, "Can God do anything," you, too, would probably say yes. But do you really believe that God can equip you with the skills, the confidence, and the ability to fulfill His plans for your life? He can. But each of us, like Sarah, has to learn to lay aside our skeptical laughter and put our faith in the One who can do anything.

"Now the Lord was gracious to Sarah as he had said, and the Lord did for Sarah what he had promised. Sarah became pregnant and bore a son to Abraham in his old age, at the very time God had promised him. Abraham gave the name Isaac to the son Sarah bore him. . . . Sarah said, 'God has brought me laughter, and everyone who hears about this will laugh with me.' And she added, 'Who would have said to Abraham that Sarah would nurse children? Yet I have borne him a son in his old age'" (Genesis 21:1-7).

The name Isaac means, "He laughs!" The Bible story of Isaac's birth ends with God, Sarah, and Abraham laughing together, sharing their joy at the impossible thing God was able to do.

Like Sarah, we may laugh at God's plan. But God laughs at our obstacles. With Him, everything is possible.

REBEKAH

A simple act of kindness can lead you to unexpected places.
Just ask Rebekah.

The late-afternoon shadows were growing long and the air was beginning to cool as the young women of Nahor went to the village well to draw water. They chatted and giggled as they walked, water jars balanced on their heads and carried at their hips. It was a peaceful time, with the day's work behind them and a chance to visit with other women as they carried out this final daily chore.

Near the well they saw a stranger resting, a traveler accompanied by 10 heavily-laden camels. The young women glanced at him as they passed, wondering quietly among themselves who this wanderer might be.

As the girls returned from the well the stranger stepped up to one of them, Rebekah, and asked for a drink of water. Rebekah brought the heavy water jar down from her head and held it out for him to drink. Glancing over at his thirsty animals, she thought of the lessons that had been drilled into her from childhood about kindness to strangers. She knew the generous offer would make her late in returning to her family, but she said to the man, "I'll draw water for your camels, too, until they've had enough to drink" (see Genesis 24:19).

It was a simple little moment of generosity—a random act of kindness, it might seem—but something was going on behind the scenes that Rebekah didn't know about, something far from random. The stranger at the well was a trusted servant of her great-uncle Abraham, a man she had never met. Abraham had moved far away from the rest of his family, following the call of God to the distant land of Canaan. Abraham's servant was here now, visiting Abraham's ancestral home, seeking a suitable and God-fearing wife for his master's son, Isaac.

Not wanting to leave anything to chance, the faithful servant made a bargain with God when he arrived on the outskirts of town. "May it be," he prayed, "that when I say to a girl, 'Please let down your jar that I may have a drink,' and she says, 'Drink, and I'll water your camels too'—let her be the one you have chosen for your servant Isaac" (Genesis 24:14).

Rebekah didn't know it, but as soon as she made her kind offer of water for the camels, she was taking her place in God's plan. A door was opening in front of her—a door to a new life that she had never imagined.

She suspected quickly that things were about to change when, as soon as the camels were watered, Abraham's servant began to load her down with valuable jewelry. He also asked if he could spend the night at her father's house and seemed delighted to learn that she was the granddaughter of Nahor, Abraham's brother.

Once Abraham's servant arrived at Rebekah's home, the whole story came out. Long-lost brother Abraham was now a powerful prince and chieftain in the land of Canaan, and his son and heir Isaac would inherit everything once the elderly patriarch died. Isaac was missing only one thing–a bride. And Abraham had insisted that his son's wife should come, not from the pagan Canaanites who lived around them, but from his own people who worshipped the true God. Abraham's servant was convinced that the God he trusted had led him straight to Rebekah and her water jar, and he promptly made an offer of marriage.

Who knows what thoughts whirled through Rebekah's mind at that moment? Was she terrified, excited, hopeful at the prospect of leaving everything familiar to travel to a strange land and marry a cousin she'd never seen? Perhaps, like most young girls, she felt a mixture of all those things as she looked into the eyes of a future she'd never dared imagine. At home, she was the daughter of a prominent and successful man in the community, but in Canaan she would live like a tribal princess, her husband one of the most powerful and wealthy men in the land. And, though she didn't know it yet, her son would continue the family line of Abraham, the family with which God had made a special covenant, the family that would someday become the nation of Israel.

And it all began with an offer of water for camels.

We don't know where our simple acts, our everyday choices, will lead. God may have a greater destiny in store for you than you can imagine at this point. Your future, like Rebekah's, may hold things you haven't even dreamed of. But how do we get from where we are now, to where God wants us to be? One simple act of obedience at a time. Be faithful to the task God is calling you to right now. Be kind to the people God places in your path today. You can never tell where a random act of kindness may lead.

Jesus told a parable in which a rich man rewarded his servant with the

How do we get from where we are now, to where God wants us to be? One simple act of obedience at a time.

words, "You have been faithful with a few things; I will put you in charge of many things." The same thing might have been said of Rebekah. She was faithful in the simple task of watering camels, showing kindness to a stranger; she became a matriarch of one of the most important families in history.

Women in those days were seldom given a choice in their marriage arrangements. Rebekah's father and brother negotiated a deal with Abraham's servant; Rebekah wasn't consulted at first. That was probably what she expected; she understood how marriage worked in her culture. But when the servant wanted to leave at once to carry her home to Isaac, Rebekah's menfolk dug their heels in. Perhaps they felt such haste was inappropriate, perhaps the girl should be given a little time to adjust to the great change in her life. "Let's ask Rebekah what she wants to do," they suggested.

"So they called Rebekah and asked her, 'Will you go with this man?'

'I will go,' she said."

Given her chance at a new life, Rebekah seized it. She was ready, even eager to move forward into the future God had planned for her.

When God shows us a small task we can do to glorify Him and bless others, remember Rebekah watering the camels. And if that small act of kindness leads to a life-changing opportunity, move forward in faith and take hold of it—just like Rebekah did.

RACHEL

Will getting your heart's desire make you happy?
Ask Rachel.

It was love at first sight. He saw her, and he could think of nothing else. She was young, beautiful, and charming. He was head-over-heels, and he had to have her.

They fell in love, and though their romance had its ups and downs, eventually they were together. Their love story lasted until she died. Yet the heroine of the Bible's most romantic love story is remembered not as the happiest woman in the Bible, but as the saddest.

Her name was Rachel. She was the younger of two daughters—the younger and the more beautiful. When her cousin Jacob came to stay, she won his heart instantly, and he immediately asked her father for her hand in marriage.

Rachel's father, Laban, knew how to drive a bargain. He knew that the young man in front of him wanted to marry Rachel very, very much. When someone wants something that badly, they're usually willing to pay. In Jacob's case, the price was steep: seven years of labor in return for Rachel as a bride.

Jacob agreed. Jacob paid. Rachel waited. Waited to be united with the man she loved; waited to begin her life as a wife and mother. For seven years she watched Jacob as he managed her father's flocks and herds, waiting for the moment he'd be hers alone.

But Rachel's father had another surprise in store. He knew he could get more work out of Jacob and still keep him dangling on a string. We don't know when he let Rachel in on the plan, but sometime before the wedding he drew Rachel aside and told her that, well, she wasn't actually going to marry Jacob. Her older sister Leah, who still hadn't had an offer of marriage, would walk down the aisle with Jacob—fully veiled so that the groom would be fooled until he found himself alone with his bride.

How did Rachel feel? Angry at her father? Sad about losing the man she loved? Jealous of her sister?

The Bible doesn't tell us. But she did go along with the plan. She probably had little choice.

Rachel sat through that wedding, probably in a separate tent away from the festivities so her presence there wouldn't give away the secret. She listened to the sound of feasting and celebration. As night fell, she imagined Jacob alone in another tent, lifting the veil, discovering Leah instead of Rachel. Rachel sat alone on the wedding night that should have been hers.

But when morning dawned, she learned that Jacob still wanted her. And when the week-long wedding celebration was over there was a second ceremony—Rachel became Jacob's second wife, in exchange for a promise of another seven years' service. A second wife was lower in status, but Rachel probably didn't care. She had the man she loved—even if she had to share him with her sister! Surely now her happily-ever-after would begin.

But the rest of Rachel's story, as it's recorded in the Bible, is no fairytale. Rachel may have had Jacob's love, but Leah had the privilege of bearing him children while Rachel remained infertile. How Rachel's heart broke as she saw Leah proudly present Jacob with one son after another! Genesis 30, verse 1 tells us: "When Rachel saw that she was not bearing Jacob any children, she became jealous of her sister. So she said to Jacob, 'Give me children, or I'll die!'"

Jacob, following the custom of his time, took two concubines as well as his two wives, and they gave him even more sons. The children born to Rachel's maidservant were counted as being Rachel's children, but she still longed to truly give Jacob a son of their own. Rachel's wish finally came true with the birth of Joseph. Yet even then she wasn't fully content. Joseph's name means "may He add," for she prayed at once for the Lord to add another son to her family. Perhaps she was still trying to catch up with Leah.

Some years later, Rachel bore a second son, but the birth was difficult and Rachel realized that she probably would not survive. With her dying breath she named the baby Ben-Oni, which meant "son of my trouble." His father Jacob renamed him Benjamin, "son of my right hand," and cherished both Joseph and Benjamin as his favored sons in memory of his beloved wife Rachel.

Rachel experienced great love in her life—the kind of passionate romance that every woman dreams of. Wouldn't most of us be thrilled to find a man who would endure 14 years of indentured servitude just to win our hand in marriage? That's true love! That's romance!

Yet that great romance didn't bring Rachel happiness. Her life from the time she met Jacob was filled with conflict, jealousy, resentment, and disappointment. Their romance was bitter-sweet. It was a love so powerful its memory lingered with Jacob long after Rachel was gone and he had only her sons to remind him of her. Yet it seemed to produce little in the way of domestic peace, harmony, and contentment. Rachel and Jacob got what they wanted—each other—yet Rachel, at least, spent the rest of her life looking for something more.

The last time Rachel's name is mentioned in the Bible is in Matthew 2:18. After the birth of Jesus, when the vindictive King Herod ordered a slaughter of the children in the city of Bethlehem, the Gospel writer quotes a passage from the book of Jeremiah: "A voice is heard in Ramah, weeping and great mourning, Rachel weeping for her children and refusing to be comforted, because they are no more." Rachel, the mother of the Jewish race, here represents all the weeping women whose sons were murdered. In her last biblical appearance, Rachel has come to stand for the unhappiness that marked her life—she is associated with women mourning for their lost children.

So often we set our hearts on the one thing we believe will make us happy, just as Jacob and Rachel set their hearts on each other. Often it's a romantic relationship that we think will make our lives complete. Or it might be something else—a job, a new home, a child. Surely, we think, when this long-awaited dream comes true we will finally know happiness.

But Rachel's story suggests otherwise. Finding your heart's desire is wonderful, but it brings only a temporary happiness. Tragedy and disaster can still shatter those dreams. True happiness comes only from trusting in God, accepting His plan for our lives, and gratefully enjoying the good things He gives us. That's a lesson Rachel may never have learned—but it's one that each of us should take to heart if we want to be remembered for joy rather than for sorrow.

MIRIAM

*Have you ever sat in church looking at a friend and thinking, She's got everything!
Why can't God bless me as He blesses her? Miriam would have understood
your thoughts—and she'd probably want you to learn from her mistake.*

She stood on the seashore, triumphant, filled with the power and presence of God's
Spirit. God had just given her people a tremendous victory, and Miriam, over-
whelmed with the joy of the moment, led the people in a song and dance of praise
(Exodus 15:19-21). It was probably the high point of her life.

Not long afterwards—a matter of months, probably—Miriam found herself an outcast
from her people, struck down with the dreaded disease of leprosy. She had been punished
by God, singled out as an example for her rebellious attitude (Numbers 12). As she stood
outside the cluster of tents, rejected and alone, she must have wondered how she had
plummeted so quickly from the heights to the depths.

Miriam's whole life had been a roller coaster ride of ups and downs. Born into slavery,
she and her family had been terrorized by the Egyptian pharoah's death threat against
Hebrew babies. Miriam was a key player in her family's plan to save her infant brother
Moses, and when the baby Moses was unexpectedly rescued by a princess, it was Miriam

who made the contact that allowed him to be nursed and cared for by his own mother (Exodus 2:1-10). Even as a young girl Miriam was clever and courageous.

But after the terror and excitement of those early years, Miriam's life sank into obscurity. For years she toiled as a slave while her brother Moses first enjoyed the privileged life of an Egyptian prince, then mysteriously disappeared. Miriam must have felt the years of her life slipping away and wondered if God would ever intervene to save His people.

Then Moses returned. Along with Miriam's other brother, Aaron, he confronted Pharaoh and demanded the release of the Hebrew slaves. God used a series of powerful miracles to demonstrate that His power was greater than that of the gods of Egypt. And Miriam found her life changed utterly. She and her family were right at the heart of what God was doing for His people.

Moses was unquestionably the leader, the one God had called, but everyone in the family was given a special role to play. Aaron was Moses' spokesman during the conflict with Pharoah. Later, he and his sons would be called to serve as priests. As for Miriam, the Bible describes her as "Miriam the prophetess" (Exodus 15:20). In ancient Israel, a prophet or prophetess was a person with a special connection to God, empowered by the Holy Spirit to carry God's message to His people. As Miriam stood on the shores of the Red Sea after the waters had swallowed up the pursuing Egyptian army, she lifted her tambourine and led the women of Israel with singing and dancing. At that moment Miriam was completely open to God's leading, ready to be used in any way He might use her.

The real victim of Miriam's envy was Miriam herself.

Why, then, do we see Miriam in such a completely different light a short time later? The answer is revealed in Numbers 12, where we learn that Miriam and Aaron grew jealous of Moses' special role as Israel's leader. In their resentment, they lashed out at an innocent party— Moses' wife. The Bible tells us they "talked against" him because he had married a Cushite, or Ethiopian— a woman of a different race, not one of the chosen people of Israel. But the in-law tension and racial slurs were only the surface manifestation of a deeper discontent. "'Has the Lord spoken only through Moses?' they asked. 'Hasn't he also spoken through us?'"

Maybe you've walked in Miriam's sandals. Your spiritual life has had some high places, points where you really felt you were in touch with God and He was able to use you. But there are low places too, and when you walk through the valleys you grow envious of those who seem to have more glamorous gifts, a more successful spiritual life and a greater share of God's blessings. You wonder why your life is so hard while theirs seems so easy. Perhaps, like Miriam, you find that envy and resentment take the form of lashing out and attacking others.

None of us wants to feel that way. We'd love to live always on a spiritual mountaintop, playing the tambourine and praising the Lord for the great things He's done. But there's a dark side to all human characters. We all hide our ugly secrets—the jealousy, resentment, and anger toward those we feel are more fortunate, more blessed.

God responded swiftly to Miriam's and Aaron's complaints. He defended Moses, and struck Miriam with leprosy for seven days, during which she was exiled from the Israelite camp. Why Miriam and not Aaron? The Bible doesn't say. Perhaps she was singled out because she was the ringleader in their resentment.

Like many of God's punishments in the Old Testament, this one might seem harsh and vindictive to our modern point of view. But it provides a striking illustration of how jealousy and resentment actually work. The real victim of Miriam's envy was not Moses or even his wife. The person who got hurt most was Miriam herself. Jealousy is destructive. Resentment is a disease that eats away at us from the inside. What Miriam experienced—sickness, fear, isolation—is what awaits any of us if we focus on how God is blessing others rather than how God has blessed us.

Miriam had been blessed by God and given a special role to play. But when she allowed resentment to cloud her vision, she closed the channel of communication between herself and God. Instead of dancing on the seashore singing songs of praise, she found herself outside the camp, diseased and bitter.

We don't know how Miriam responded to her bout with leprosy, although the fact that she was restored to the community suggests that she repented and was forgiven. She never appears again in the Bible story. It would be so much nicer to remember Miriam—the first woman in the Bible to be called a prophetess—as that triumphant singer on the seashore, filled with God's Spirit, obedient to His call, secure in her place among God's people. But the rest of Miriam's story teaches that even those of us who dance on the mountaintop can descend to the valley; even women whose lives have been powerfully touched by God can still be consumed by resentment, anger, and jealousy. Only as we keep our eyes on God and focus on our own connection with Him can we continue to keep in step with the triumphant dance in which He leads us all.

The Daughters of ZELOPHEHAD

*When you feel as if everything's stacked against you
and there's no way you can beat the system—
a team of sisters from the ancient world might have some advice for you.*

Have you ever heard the expression, "You can't fight City Hall"? We usually use it to mean that you can't fight forces that are too strong for you—government, bureaucracy, a system that's set in its ways. It can apply to futile attempts to create change in your community, your workplace—maybe even your church. When you try to propose a new idea and someone says, "But we've never done it that way before!" you can feel like you've hit a brick wall. Your voice isn't being heard and sure enough, "You can't fight City Hall."

Five sisters in ancient Israel came up against that kind of unstoppable wall. They were among those whose families had left Egyptian slavery and traveled into the desert with Moses the great liberator. But their father, Zelophehad, died in the desert, and he left behind him no sons, just five daughters.

In ancient times, having no sons was a disaster. In most cultures of the time family property was passed down to sons. Daughters became part of their husband's family, often taking with them an expensive dowry from their fathers. Daughters were an expense, a drain on the family economy. But sons could safeguard your fortune and your family name for generations to come.

By the standards of their society, these five women—Mahlah, Noah, Hoglah, Milcah and Tirzah—were women without any property or any rights. Their father was dead, they had no brothers, and they were not yet married. Husbands would have been able to speak on the sisters' behalf, but these young women were left not only without a father and a protector, but also without a voice. Their words had no value—because society viewed them as having no value.

What a devastating situation! Zelophehad's daughters could have sat down, thrown up their hands in despair, and wept about the terrible fate that had left them fatherless, brotherless, husbandless, and landless. Maybe they did sit down and cry. But at some point, one of them must have had an idea.

"Let's go to Moses," one of the sisters might have said. "Let's tell him our situation. Maybe he'll hear us, and do something about it."

Perhaps one or more of her other sisters had doubts. They knew men in power didn't usually listen to powerless women. Law and tradition were against them. How could they fight City Hall?

City Hall in those days was Moses' Tent of Meeting. Somehow all the sisters must have come to an agreement, because one day all five of them showed up in front of Moses and explained their situation. We don't know which sister did the talking, but their words were recorded for all time in Numbers 27:3, 4.

"Our father died in the desert . . . and left no sons. Why should our father's name disappear from his clan because he had no son? Give us property among our father's relatives."

No doubt these women felt nervous, making such an unprecedented request. Their hearts may have beat a little harder as the spokeswoman among them placed their case before the great leader, Moses. But the God they trusted in came through for them. Numbers 27:5-7, tells us:

"Moses brought their case before the Lord and the Lord said to him, 'What Zelophehad's daughters are saying is right. You must certainly give them property as an inheritance among their father's relatives and turn their father's inheritance over to them.'"

In fact, the courage of these women changed not only their own situation, but that of other women as well. As a result of Zelophehad's daughters, the inheritance laws of Israel were written to ensure that if a man died without sons, his property would be inherited by his daughters.

This tiny story takes up only a few verses in biblical history. It seems less like a story of great spiritual significance, than a footnote explaining a clause in Israelite property law. What does it say to women in the twenty-first century?

We all find ourselves up against "City Hall" at times—against systems and situations that appear unjust and unchangeable. We've all had the experience of being told that we can't change things, that our voice doesn't count, that we should just be quiet and accept things as we are.

But God's people can't always do that. Whether the injustice is directed at ourselves or at someone else, when we see it, we are called to do something about it. That can be scary. It can draw criticism. But the example of Mahlah, Noah, Hoglah, Milcah and Tirzah gives us hope—and also some good advice.

First, when faced with a seemingly impossible situation, trust God. He is on the side of justice and fairness and He will work behind the scenes as He did when Moses brought the plea of Zelophehad's daughters to Him.

Second, don't be afraid to speak out. Yes, you may be misunderstood or criticized. Yes, you may sometimes feel like you're trying to break through a brick wall of insensitivity, tradition, and custom. But remember that God's people throughout history—even Jesus Himself—faced those same barriers and took the risk of standing up for what was right.

Finally, take your sisters with you. Seek the support, love, and prayers of those who care about you and believe in you. Zelophehad's daughters were like five fingers curled together in an unbeatable fist—together they were far stronger than any one of them would have been alone. You aren't alone. Reach out to your God-given sisterhood of support.

The Bible records the names of hundreds and hundreds of men. We find pages and pages of genealogies recording the names of fathers and sons for hundreds of years. Only a few dozen women's names are sprinkled among those stories. Most women lived and died without their names ever being recorded or remembered. It was the custom at that time. The role of women in public life was small, and their names were forgotten.

Not the daughters of Zelophehad. We know little about their later lives, except that they agreed to marry men from their own tribe so that their father's inheritance would remain within the clan. Yet the names of all five have been preserved forever in the pages of Scripture, not just here in Numbers 27 where their story is told, but in several different places. Maybe it is God's reminder that a woman who dares to stand up and speak out will be heard—and remembered.

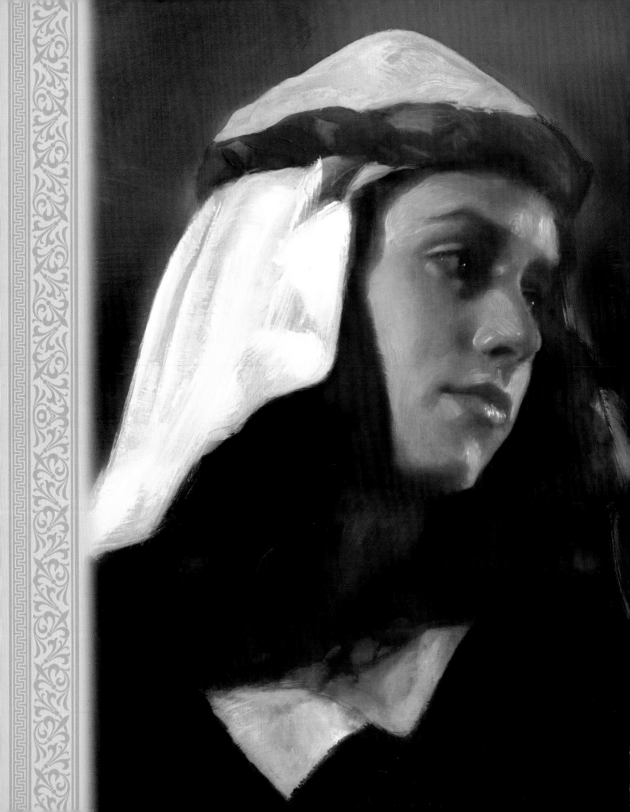

RAHAB

Taking a small step of faith can take a lot of courage.

In a country teetering on the brink of war, a woman faces a choice. She can remain loyal to her own side, or run the risk of helping the enemy. The city in which she lives is powerful and well-defended. An enemy attack will probably fail. There's little reason for this woman to throw in her lot with the would-be invaders. Her best bet is to remain a loyal, law-abiding citizen of Jericho.

Yet when the Jericho police came pounding on Rahab's door looking for two Hebrew spies, Rahab didn't turn in the spies to them. Instead, she hid them on her roof and lied about where they had gone. Why did she risk her own safety and security for a couple of random strangers?

Rahab herself makes her reason clear when she tells the spies what she has done for them: "I know that the Lord has given this land to you and that a great fear of you has fallen on us, so that all who live in this country are melting in fear because of you. We have heard how the Lord dried up the water of the Red Sea for you when you came out of Egypt . . . When we heard of it, our hearts sank and everyone's courage failed because of you, for the Lord your God is God in heaven above and on the earth below" (Joshua 2:9-11).

Rahab took a risk, defied the law, and hid the spies because she had heard amazing things about their God. Because of the stories flying around Canaan at the time, she believed that the God of Israel was powerful and mighty. She didn't know much about this God, but she wanted to throw in her lot with what she believed would be the winning side.

Common sense would argue that in a confrontation between the nomadic Hebrews and the strong walled city of Jericho, the Hebrews would be easily defeated. But Rahab had heard the tales of the exodus from Egypt, the parting of the Red Sea, and the other mighty miracles God had worked in the wilderness. On the strength of what she'd heard about Israel's God, she was willing to risk not only her own safety, but that of all her family. That was the price she demanded from the spies in return for her silence: when they captured the city of Jericho, Rahab and her entire extended family would be saved.

The spies agreed. They told Rahab to hang a scarlet cord in the same window through which she let them escape. On the day they captured Jericho, if they saw the red cord in the window, they would save Rahab and her family from the city's destruction.

How often has God called you to take a risk for Him? Have you been given the opportunity to do something that might earn you disapproval or even punishment, just because you followed God's will and did the right thing? How did you respond?

We often admire the faith of those who are willing to take risks. Like Rahab hiding the Hebrew spies, in the 1940s many European Christians took their lives into their hands by hiding Jews from the Nazis. I've often imagined myself in the shoes of someone like Corrie Ten Boom or Raoul Wallenberg. Would I help innocent people if it meant placing my own safety at risk? Or would I fade into the woodwork, collaborate with the evil government, and refuse to put myself in danger?

We can never know until we face a crisis situation how we might respond. On the afternoon before the spies came, if you'd asked Rahab whether she would defy her own king in order to protect Hebrew spies, she might not have known the answer. But when the crisis came, she was ready. She made her choice; she hung out her red cord.

Very few of us have to make the kind of life-or-death risks faced by Rahab in Jericho, or by those who befriended Jews in Nazi-occupied Europe. But every day we face choices. God calls each of us to take risks for Him. There's the risk of loving someone else when we know we might get hurt. The risk of standing up for what we believe is right in the face of ridicule. The risk of using our talents for Him even though others may not understand or appreciate what we're doing.

What holds us back from taking a risk? Fear is usually the biggest culprit. It doesn't have to be fear of prison or death. For most of us, the fear of shame, ridicule, or disapproval may be all it takes. We struggle both with fear of failure and fear of success. Fear stands between us and the things God calls us to accomplish.

What drives us forward? What can inspire us to step out in faith, to hang the red cord in our windows? The same thing that inspired Rahab. Rahab was driven to help the spies despite the risk, because she had heard great things about their God. The more we know about God and His power, the more we will be willing to risk for Him.

Against all odds, Rahab believed that the God of the Hebrews had the power to deliver the mighty, walled city of Jeri-

Fear stands between us and the things God calls us to accomplish.

cho into the hands of this rag-tag army of escaped slaves. She had heard the stories of His miracles, the powerful ways in which He delivered His people. Rahab didn't know much about those Hebrews and their God, but she knew which side she wanted to be on. She gambled on the God who had parted the Red Sea and led slaves out of Egypt, who had sent manna in the wilderness and brought water from the rock.

Do you know enough about the power of God to trust Him in your own life? Can you take the risk of believing that if you do the right thing, God will reward you?

As you look at the circumstances surrounding you today, success and victory may seem like a long shot. Just like making the walls of Jericho fall by marching around them was a long shot. But it happened, because God had promised it would. The Bible records what happened on that day when the Hebrew army marched into the ruins of Jericho:

"The young men who had done the spying went in and brought out Rahab, her father and mother and brothers and all who belonged to her. . . . Then they burned the whole city and everything in it. . . . But Joshua spared Rahab . . . with her family and all who belonged to her, because she hid the men Joshua had sent as spies to Jericho—and she lives among the Israelites to this day" (Joshua 6:23-25).

Rahab trusted a God she barely knew—enough to hang a red cord in her window as a sign of her faith. Can you do the same?

DEBORAH

Have you ever felt that God has called you to do something unexpected?
Something that may be outside your abilities?
Something others may not accept or understand?
Deborah would have known just how you feel.

Midday sun beats down on a dry, dusty path. Hot and tired, the travelers are relieved to see a patch of greenery ahead. They look forward to the rest that will come at the end of their journey when they can enjoy the shade of the great spreading tree and the cool water nearby. More than anything, though, they look forward to the spiritual refreshing that awaits them.

God-fearing men in an ancient land where few could read and write, the travelers looked to the Lord's messengers to tell them the stories of their people's past and give them hope for the future. Wise leaders of the past—men like Moses, Joshua, and Caleb—had not only interpreted God's law but also provided guidance for daily living. Now a new messenger had set up camp under this famous tree near the well-traveled roadside. This messenger claimed to have words from God to share with a people desperately in need of guidance.

But there was something unexpected. Even though the travelers knew what they'dfind before they were arrived, they were still a little surprised at what they saw. For there, beneath the palm tree, sharing words of wisdom with those who came looking for help, was—a woman.

The woman was Deborah. The Bible tells us that she was "a prophetess, the wife of Lappidoth, [who] was leading Israel at that time. She held court under the Palm of Deborah between Ramah and Bethel in the hill country of Ephraim, and the Israelites came to her to have their disputes decided" (Judges 4:4, 5).

Why was Deborah's role so unusual? Though the Bible mentions one woman who was a prophet before Deborah's time (Miriam, the sister of Moses; see Exodus 15:20), Deborah is the first and only woman described as a "leader" or "judge" of ancient Israel. She is the first woman we see in a leadership role in the Bible. God called Deborah to her task in a society where women were expected to tend the home and care for the children. Few women ever ventured outside that role. Most men had little respect for a woman's wisdom, and for men to look up to a woman as their leader and judge was almost unthinkable.

I wonder what Deborah thought when God called her to become His messenger and a leader in Israel? The Bible tells us nothing about the beginning of Deborah's journey. We don't know how God called her. We can only assume that, unusual as the call was, she responded willingly.

As Deborah first moved into that challenging, unfamiliar role, she probably didn't guess that God had an even bigger task in store for her. The nation of Israel over which Deborah ruled as a judge was experiencing difficult times. A powerful enemy king oppressed the Hebrew tribes, stealing their land and forcing them into subjection. At God's inspiration, Deborah called on a powerful Israelite chieftain, a soldier named Barak, to lead the men of Israel in a fight to regain their freedom.

But Barak hesitated. He wanted to be assured of victory. He told Deborah, "If you go with me, I will go; but if you don't go with me, I won't go" (Judges 4:8). Deborah went into battle with Barak, and their armies won a huge victory, driving back the forces of oppression.

What Israelite wife and mother of those days would ever have imagined herself marching at the head of a rebel army, leading men into battle? It was an unthinkable role for a woman. Yet as Deborah responded to God's call, He led her into unexpected places. He took the gift and talents He had given her and challenged her to use them in ways she had never imagined. Responding to that call must have taken incredible courage and trust in God. But Deborah did it.

Can you relate to Deborah? Do you feel God is calling you to serve Him in ways that may be, frankly, a little frightening? There's an old saying that assures us: "God does not call the qualified: He qualifies the called."

We often feel unqualified for the tasks God invites us to do. Those tasks might involve taking an unpopular public stand on a controversial issue, or taking a frontline role in meeting a need in your community. God's call might require you to shed your shyness and speak in front of your women's group or your congregation. God may be calling you to be faithful in a difficult family situation or to stand up for what you know is right even though friends and co-workers don't honor your convictions. Perhaps God is calling you, like Deborah, to take on a task for Him that others may question or disapprove of.

God's heroines and heroes of faith knew what it meant to be unqualified for God's call. Some of His greatest prophets—men like Moses and Jeremiah—questioned God when He called them, wondering if they had the qualifications required (Exodus 3 and 4; Jeremiah 1:6, 7).

Was Deborah afraid? Did she doubt whether she was qualified enough to be a prophetess and judge? The Bible doesn't record her inner thoughts. Yet any woman, even the most confident, would have been surprised to be pulled from her accepted role and thrust into a position of such authority.

Though God called Deborah to fill what was then considered a man's role, He drew upon her female talents and strengths. In the biblical poem that describes Deborah's accomplishments — a poem this multitalented woman herself may have composed—Deborah describes herself as "a mother in Israel." Her ability to nurture, to care for others, and to make wise decisions was cultivated in her home as she reared her own children. When God called her to be a mother to an entire nation, she was able to take those same strengths and gifts and use them in a far larger field.

God has a call for each one of us today. He has a call for you. It may be a leadership position in the public eye, like Deborah's. It may be a quiet, behind-the-scenes role that makes a great work possible. Whatever your task, you will probably have moments when you wonder, "Can I do it? Am I talented enough, strong enough, brave enough? What if people don't understand? What if they disapprove?"

When God's call seems like too much of a challenge, think of Deborah. Imagine a wife and mother who finds herself marching to battle at the head of God's army. God's call can, indeed, lead us to unexpected places. But we never go there alone. He calls us; He qualifies us. And He is with us, every step of the way.

NAOMI

How often have you been told that you must have a positive attitude to succeed?
Of course an optimistic outlook helps, but you may have found it impossible
to stay cheerful and upbeat when battered by life's trials.
If so, you're not alone. Naomi felt the same way.

To say that things hadn't worked out for Naomi would be an understatement. Famine drove her family from their homeland. As refugees in a foreign country, they were unfamiliar with the customs and language. But they adapted. They survived, as refugees always have.

Then the first blow fell. Naomi's husband died. Far from home, she was suddenly a widow with two sons to feed and care for. The boys, being young and adaptable, made themselves at home in the culture of Moab and eventually married local girls. For a brief time, Naomi's life was full again, with her sons, daughters-in-law, and the promise of grandchildren to come.

But tragedy struck a second time. Both Naomi's sons died. Without warning, she and her daughters-in-law were three widows in a society where a woman needed a man's protection to survive. Without husbands or sons, they had no income, no status, and no future. Naomi experienced the bitter grief of a mother burying her only two children. She also experienced the powerless feeling of a woman who has lost her role, her identity, and her hopes for the future.

When Naomi decided to return to her home in Israel, her daughters-in-law wanted to come with her. But she urged them to stay in Moab and marry again. They were still young; they still had hopes of starting over. "It is more bitter for me than for you," Naomi told the young women, Ruth and Orpah, "because the Lord's hand has gone out against me!" (Ruth 1:13).

Even in our darkest hours, even when we despair, as long as we remain open to His leading, He will still bless.

Naomi didn't have a positive attitude. She believed God had turned against her. As far as she could see, her life was a sinking ship and Ruth and Orpah would be smart to jump ship as soon as possible.

Today we hear a lot about the power of positive thinking. TV shows, women's magazines, motivational speakers, even Christian preachers tell us that if we face life with an optimistic, positive outlook, things will get better for us. In its most extreme form, this philosophy preaches that if we visualize positive outcomes for ourselves—"name it and claim it," as the Christian version goes—good things are guaranteed to happen.

There weren't many motivational speakers walking around Israel or Moab in 1100 B.C. Life for these people, as in many countries today, was a matter of basic survival. No one had leisure time for self-help books and life coaching. Most people—the Hebrews as well as the pagans—believed that if things went well it was a sign that your gods were blessing you. If you suffered hardship and pain, the gods had turned their backs or were punishing you for your sins.

Naomi certainly subscribed to that popular belief. Famine, exile, loss of her husband and sons—it all added up to a bleak picture. She didn't bother trying to put a positive spin on it. When she arrived back in her hometown of Bethlehem accompanied by her most persistent daughter-in-law, Ruth, Naomi made things pretty clear.

"Don't call me Naomi," she told her former neighbors. "Call me Mara, because the Almighty has made my life very bitter. I went away full, but the Lord has brought me back empty. Why call me Naomi? The Lord has afflicted me; the Almighty has brought misfortune upon me" (Ruth 1:20, 21).

Naomi rejected her name, which meant "pleasant." Names carried a great deal of meaning in her culture, and seeking for a new name that reflected her current circumstances, she chose Mara, which meant bitter.

Naomi was bitter. Naomi was negative. She had a bad attitude. By every modern standard of success, Naomi was destined to fail.

But the rest of the book of Ruth tells a different story. Back home in Bethlehem, Naomi helps Ruth come up with a plan to support them by gleaning leftover grain from the fields while capturing the attention of Boaz, the rich man who owns the field. Naomi watches over the relationship, encouraging Ruth and giving her motherly advice. By the end of the story Ruth and Boaz are married, the family fortune is redeemed, and Naomi finally holds a grandson in her arms. The women of Bethlehem—who never did get into the habit of calling her Mara—congratulate Naomi on how God has blessed her.

"The women said to Naomi: 'Praise be to the Lord, who this day has not left you without a kinsman-redeemer.'

"Then Naomi took the child, laid him in her lap and cared for him. The women living there said, 'Naomi has a son.'" (Ruth 4:14, 16, 17).

Naomi left Bethlehem full—full of family, full of hope—and returned empty. But the Lord filled her heart and her home once again. And He did it despite her despair and discouragement.

Yes, a positive attitude is a wonderful thing. Despite their lack of motivational speakers and self-help books, the Bible writers recognized the value of positive thinking. The author of Proverbs tells us that "A cheerful heart is good medicine, but a crushed spirit dries up the bones." Jesus commended those who came to Him with faith, telling them that their faith contributed to their healing (see Luke 8:48; 17:19). A basic knowledge of human psychology tells us that positive, optimistic people are more likely to succeed than those who go around town announcing, "Call me Bitter! God has turned His back on me!"

The problem is that we don't always feel positive and optimistic. We all have our "Mara" days. Women who have suffered multiple losses, who have survived abuse, who struggle with chronic illness or depression, may find it especially hard to produce that happy, optimistic attitude. And our culture sends the message that if you can't feel happy, if you can't produce hope and optimism like a rabbit from a magician's hat, you can't be blessed.

Naomi's story affirms a different truth. Yes, hope and optimism are wonderful things. But they're human things. They depend on transient qualities like our physical and mental health, or our outward circumstances. God's goodness comes from outside ourselves. God's blessings depend on His nature, not on ours.

On the days when we feel like "Mara," when we feel God has turned His back, when we can't muster an optimistic thought to save our lives—God is still there. He still cares, whether we're optimists or pessimists, whether we feel like being called Naomi or Mara. Even in our darkest hours, even when we despair, as long as we remain open to His leading, He will still bless.

If you woke up this morning full of life, energy and hope for the future— congratulations! Use that positive attitude to bless to others. But if this is a "Mara" day—if you feel discouraged, bitter, even hopeless—don't give up. You may feel that God has turned His back, but He hasn't. He's still there, and He loves Mara just as much as Naomi, pessimists just as much as optimists.

Noami

HANNAH

Can you imagine receiving your heart's desire . . . only to give it away?

Lord, please hear me! I'm desperate. All I want in this world is a child. Can you answer my prayer, and give me a baby?"

How many women throughout history have prayed that prayer? Even today, in the age of reproductive technologies that were science fiction only a generation ago, women still pray for the gift of a new life, a baby of their own. And that prayer has been rising to God's throne since the beginning of time.

More than 3,000 years ago a woman prayed that prayer. Her life was as different from yours and mine as it's possible to imagine. She was one of two wives in a polygamous marriage. She had no education. She lived as a peasant scratching a subsistence living from the soil, bringing animal sacrifices to worship her God. Her life was utterly unlike yours or mine—except that her plea for a child rings fresh in the ears of every woman who has ever struggled with infertility.

"And she made a vow, saying, 'O Lord Almighty, if you will only look upon your servant's misery and remember me, and not forget your servant but give her a son, then I will give him to the Lord for all the days of his life'" (1 Samuel 1:11).

Hannah's prayer was answered. She left the Lord's tabernacle that day assured that God would give her the long-awaited son, and nine months later baby Samuel was born.

But Hannah's story doesn't end with Samuel's miracle birth. No doubt when she prayed for a child, Hannah's dreams of the future involved her little boy growing up in her home, learning at her knee. But when Hannah vowed to give her child back to the Lord, she took that vow seriously.

When Samuel was weaned—probably at about 3 years of age—Hannah brought him to live at the temple under the care of the high priest, Eli. From then on she visited him only once a year, when she came for the annual festival. Each year she brought tangible evidence of a mother's love—a little hand-made robe. (You can read the whole story in 1 Samuel 1 and 2.) Hannah, granted the wonderful gift of a child, laid aside her own dreams and plans for that child in order to give him back to God.

This story takes my breath away. What mother, especially one who has faced infertility and been granted a "miracle child," could give up her 3-year-old to be raised far from home, her only contact a yearly visit? Even though the Lord blessed Hannah and her husband with five more children, her firstborn must always have held a special place in her heart.

I cannot imagine leaving either of my children to be raised by someone else, far away from me. As Christians, God calls us to put Him first—ahead of all earthly ties and connections. But sometimes those relationships—to children, to parents, to spouses and friends—seem so much more real and powerful than our commitment to God. Could I give up anything—even my loved ones—if God required it of me?

I don't believe that Hannah's and Samuel's situation is meant to be the norm for parents and children. God's call for most parents is to raise their own children in their own home. But in another way, Hannah shows all of us the pattern for how we are to regard even our most intimate relationships.

God gave Samuel to Hannah. But Hannah had to be willing to give Samuel back to God. She had to accept that Samuel was not hers; he was God's.

It's in the nature of human love to want to grab on and hold tight. We believe on some level that our children, our spouses, our parents, and siblings, are actually ours—that we have a right to them. Human love wants to possess another person.

But the people we love—even our own children—are individuals, created by God, belonging only to Him. We have the privilege of loving them and caring for them for awhile. But that's all.

I remember the haunting words of a popular song that played on the airwaves when I was younger. It reminded listeners that "The hardest part of love . . . is letting go." Letting go was hard for Hannah. Imagine how many tears were stitched into the fabric of that homespun robe she brought to the tabernacle each year.

Truly loving the people whom God has placed in our lives means being willing to let go. It means recognizing that each of them has a relationship with God, and a destiny planned by God, that is unique to them. It may mean giving up our cherished dreams about how our lives, and others' lives, should work out—and accepting that we're not in control. God is.

A good friend of mine had a baby daughter who, at about 1 year old, began to show signs of a severe developmental disorder. My friend describes how she spent the next year wearing herself to exhaustion with her daughter's treatments and therapies. "I was determined I was going to make her normal," she recalls now. "Then one day, when she was about 2, I just gave up. I said to God, 'You gave her to me. Now I'm giving her back to You. I love her and I'll care for her as long as she lives, but she's Yours.' I accepted that I couldn't make her into the normal child I wanted her to be."

As we give up our desire to manage the future for ourselves, our empty hands are open to accept all that God has for us.

Sixteen years later, my friend is the happy mother of a well-cared-for, severely disabled teenager. When she gave up her dream of a having a "normal" child and her attempt to control her daughter's future, she was able to give her back to God as Hannah did, and accept the unique blessings of raising a disabled child.

Not all our dreams come true. Many infertile women never know the joy of holding a baby. Many single women long to marry a caring partner, but never find one. Some mothers weep for children who suffer illness or disability, or for those who make destructive choices. Hannah's story challenges us all to learn the hardest part of love—letting go. As we give up our dreams and our desire to manage the future for ourselves and our loved ones, our empty hands are open to accept all that God has for us. Like Hannah, who sang a beautiful hymn of praise after leaving Samuel at the tabernacle, we can say:

"My heart rejoices in the Lord; in the Lord my horn is lifted high" (1 Samuel 2:1).

ABIGAIL

*How can you cope in a marriage that's less than perfect?
Abigail might have had some good advice.*

Probably hers was an arranged marriage. Most were in the place and time where she lived. She didn't have any choice in the man her parents chose for her, but no doubt, like most young girls she hoped that her husband-to-be would be handsome, gentle, and kind.

Her hope was disappointed. Whether he was unkind and mean-spirited from the beginning, or whether his unpleasant traits showed up later in the marriage, we don't know. What the Bible does tell us is that Abigail, an "intelligent and beautiful" woman, was married to Nabal, who was "surly and mean in his dealings" (1 Samuel 25:3).

So Abigail, like many a woman before and after her, found herself yoked for life to a man she could neither love nor respect. In fact, few people had any respect for Nabal, including his own servants. He was a rich man. In a time when wealth was measured in livestock, the Bible tells us that Nabal had 1,000 goats and 3,000 sheep, but he was spiritually and emotionally impoverished.

Abigail would have lived out her life unhappy, unknown, and unrecorded to history if it hadn't been for her husband's encounter with a young desperado named David. At the time, David was an outlaw, the leader of a ragtag group of men little better than bandits, who hired themselves out as mercenaries to anyone who would pay. But if David's present life was unimpressive, he had a striking future ahead of him. He was destined to become Israel's greatest king—a fact he already knew, for it had been prophesied from his boyhood. At this point, David was down and out, but there were better days ahead.

The latest job David and his men had taken on involved providing protection for Nabal's shepherds while they were out in the hills watching those huge flocks. The job went well, but when David came at sheep-shearing time to collect pay for himself and his men, Nabal treated him with the same churlish disrespect he showed everyone. "Who is this David?" Nabal asked cynically. "Why should I take my bread and water, and the meat I have slaughtered for my shearers, and give it to men coming from who knows where?" (1 Samuel 25:10, 11). Nabal's shepherds confirmed that David's men had indeed protected them, but Nabal refused to listen or offer compensation.

Maybe you can guess how Abigail felt at that point. Maybe you've experienced how it feels to be embarrassed by the behavior of someone close to you. Many women can tell stories about feeling publicly shamed by the behavior or their husband or another close family member. Perhaps you're one of those women.

And perhaps, like Abigail, you understand that sometimes it goes deeper than just shame. Nabal's refusal to provide for David and his men did more than just make Nabal look bad. It also put Nabal's family at risk. David had what amounted to a private army, and a feud with a man like David could easily lead to bloodshed. This was more than just speculation. David actually threatened to attack Nabal's household. "It's been useless," David said, "all my watching over this fellow's property in the desert so that nothing of his was missing. He has paid me back evil for good. May God deal with David, be it ever so severely, if by morning I leave alive one male of all who belong to him!" (1 Samuel 25:21, 22).

At this point, Abigail took matters into her own hands. She didn't bother confronting Nabal. She knew he wouldn't listen. Instead, she herself authorized the servants to bring a generous amount of food to David's camp. Abigail followed on a donkey and bowed before David, apologizing for her husband's rudeness and offering the food she had brought as payment for David's service. Then she begged David not to take revenge upon her husband and household.

Abigail's story has an almost fairytale ending. When she returns home and tells Nabal what she's done, he is stricken and becomes "like a stone," presumably from anger or shock. Ten days later he dies. David then sends for Abigail and marries her himself; she becomes the second wife of Israel's future king.

Not every unhappy marriage ends in such a fairy tale fashion. Unkind and unreliable husbands don't always die conveniently, and princes-to-be don't ride up every day with offers of marriage. Yet Abigail's story can still offer hope for a woman trapped in an unhappy relationship, shamed and even endangered by her husband's actions.

Abigail never lost her dignity even though Nabal had no respect for her or for others. In her encounters with David she was poised and gracious, respectful of both herself and of him. Though she apologized for her husband's behavior, she made no excuses for him, frankly telling David that Nabal had behaved foolishly. But she never attacked Nabal or lowered herself to his level. Rather, she did what she knew was right, what had to be done to protect her family and household.

Many modern-day Abigails suffer because of a selfish or uncaring spouse, a man they simply cannot respect. It's easy to get bogged down in a never-ending conflict with such a person, but this accomplishes nothing. Attacking him only drags you down to his level. Abigail knew that she couldn't change Nabal. The only thing she could do was to act rightly in spite of what he did wrong. Abigail made the choice to be responsible for herself and her own actions, to continue to respond with dignity and grace, even though she was caught in a situation that might easily have robbed her of all self-respect. She didn't allow Nabal, or her unhappy marriage, to define her. Instead, she took upon herself the responsibility for doing the right thing.

Abigail's story can offer hope for a woman trapped in an unhappy relationship, shamed and even endangered by her husband's actions.

Maybe you're living in a relationship that's less than picture-perfect. That doesn't mean you're powerless. God has given you, as He gave Abigail, the ability to make your own choices about how you'll respond. You can't change your husband, but you can change your own actions. You can choose to act with creativity, grace, and dignity in a difficult situation, just as Abigail did. And you can trust God that your future holds better days ahead—just as Abigail's did.

BATHSHEBA

Ever felt like your life was out of control?
Bathsheba would understand.

One fine spring day about 3,000 years ago, a woman took a bath. Millennia have rolled by since then, great civilizations have risen and fallen, but most women still enjoy a nice bath. I enjoy a hot bubble bath, with some candles and soft music if I really want to relax. Bathsheba enjoyed hers outdoors on the roof, as many people of her time did——a refreshing retreat on a hot Jerusalem day.

Bathsheba's house wasn't far from King David's palace. The king, out walking on his own roof, looked down and saw Bathsheba. The Bible tells us: "The woman was very beautiful, and David sent someone to find out about her. The man said, 'Isn't this Bathsheba, the daughter of Eliam and the wife of Uriah the Hittite?'" (2 Samuel 11:2, 3).

For the king of Israel, the leader of God's chosen people, that should have been the end of the story. David knew that being the wife of another man put Bathsheba off limits, no matter how lovely she looked in her rooftop spa.

But the problem with having power is that you get used to getting whatever you want. And for a king in ancient times that included having any woman you wanted. David already had several wives, but apparently a harem wasn't enough for him. He saw Bathsheba; he wanted Bathsheba. 2 Samuel 11:4 succinctly tells the rest of the story.

"Then David sent messengers to get her. She came to him, and he slept with her. . . . Then she went back home."

The romance is over in a single verse. The king's messengers came knocking at Bathsheba's door with a command: "The king wants you. Come with us to the palace." She came. He slept with her. She went home. Delivered back to her own doorstep like a package the king no longer needed.

What about Bathsheba? As is so often the case with women in Bible stories, there's not a word here to tell us how she felt. Some Bible commentators have suggested that Bathsheba deliberately positioned her bath where she could be seen from the king's roof, hoping to attract royal attention. Possibly, but there's no hint of it in the Bible text. Bathsheba may have had nothing more seductive on her mind than a good soak in the tub. Whatever her intentions, events quickly moved out of her control.

Saying "No, thanks," wasn't really an option when a king asked you to accompany him to the royal bedchamber—not if you wanted to stay alive. Who knows what thoughts were on Bathsheba's mind that night–or the following morning when she was sent back to her own house? Did King David offer her gifts? Money? Promises of future meetings? Was she excited by the attention, or terrified that her soldier husband, away at war, would find out?

Whatever Bathsheba felt, it's pretty certain she didn't feel in control of the situation. David was king. He held all the power. And within a short time, Bathsheba realized she was pregnant.

She sent a message to the king to let him know what was going on. With her husband away in battle, there was no way she could pretend the baby was his. She'd be exposed as an adulteress unless the king agreed to protect her.

King David had a plan all right, but it was a typical example of one wrong deed leading to another. First he arranged for Uriah, Bathsheba's husband, to come home from the battlefield for a few nights. But Uriah refused to enjoy the comforts of his own home and his wife's company while his comrades were in the field. Though he obeyed the king's summons to Jerusalem, he slept at the palace with the king's guard. And so there was no chance of convincing Uriah that the baby was his.

At David's next step, Bathsheba surely realized events had spun out of control. For King David sent word to his army commander to put Uriah in the thick of the next battle and then withdraw the men around him—guaranteeing that Uriah would be killed in combat. Then, as soon as a decent interval had passed, David brought Bathsheba to the palace and married her. Her son would now be born as a legitimate son of the king.

But even worse things were ahead for Bathsheba. Her child lived only a few days after birth, and a prophet told King David that the child's death was punishment for the sin he and Bathsheba had committed.

How devastated Bathsheba must have been! The life she had enjoyed just a few months ago was in pieces. Her husband was dead, her child was dead, and she was one of King David's many wives, probably looked down upon by the other wives because hers was a "love match" rather than a powerful political alliance like some of theirs. Her life had been completely uprooted because of a king's lust, his ability to demand obedience, and his control over the lives of those around them. While Bathsheba wasn't entirely blameless, she was certainly not in control of what happened to her.

The Bible tells us that David repented of his sin and returned to God. Psalm 51 is a beautiful prayer of repentance in which King David begs God to wash his heart clean.

We don't know about Bathsheba's repentance, about the tears she cried, about how she went on with her life after the events recorded in 2 Samuel 11. The next time she appears in the Bible, King David is an old man, ready to die. Bathsheba has borne him four sons, and he has promised that the eldest of these, Solomon, will be his heir and rule the kingdom after him. Amid the turbulent power play surrounding the death of an old king with many ambitious sons, Bathsheba went to David's deathbed to remind of his promise. King David kept that promise: Bathsheba's son Solomon inherited the throne after David's death.

We all face situations where we have the power to change things, where we require only God-given courage and determination to act. But we also face times in life when we're like Bathsheba. We find ourselves at the mercy of events beyond our control, our lives uprooted by other people's decisions and mistakes. Like Bathsheba, we may not be blameless, but neither are we powerful enough to put all the pieces back together.

When we're not strong enough to take control, remember that God is. God ultimately had a plan for Bathsheba that involved putting her son on the throne of Israel. We're not in control; God is. And the God who is in control loves us and has our best interests at heart, if we'll just place ourselves in His hands.

The Widow of ZAREPHATH

When you feel you have nothing left to give . . .
God calls you to take a step of faith.

Have you ever been at the end of your rope? Maybe you've been in a situation where you felt, either literally or symbolically, that you had nothing left to give. A widowed woman in a town called Zarephath felt that way. Times were hard, famine stalked the land, and with a child to support and no man to protect and provide for her, this woman fared worse than most. She and her son were literally at the point of starvation.

One day she went out to gather a few sticks to build a fire. She had nothing left in the house except a jar with a handful of flour in the bottom and jug with a few drops of oil. She planned to bake them into a small piece of bread then share the meal with her son. It might be the last meal they would ever eat. Beyond that she had no plans, no hope.

As she gathered sticks near the town gate, a strange man approached her. "Would you bring me a little water in a jar so I may have a drink?" he asked her.

She could do that much. Going to get water, she stopped as the stranger called out a second request. "And bring me, please, a piece of bread" (1 Kings 17:10, 11).

She turned back to explain why she couldn't supply the man with bread. She told him exactly what her situation was: she was down to her last bit of flour and oil, ready to make her last meal and then starve to death.

The stranger, who was a prophet of God, didn't offer comfort, or hope, or practical help. He didn't even offer to pray for her. Instead, he offered her a promise wrapped inside a challenge.

"Elijah said to her, 'Don't be afraid. Go home and do as you have said. But first make a small cake of bread for me from what you have and bring it to me, and then make something for yourself and your son. For this is what the Lord, the God of Israel, says: "The jar of flour will not be used up and the jug of oil will not run dry until the day the Lord gives rain on the land."'" (1 Kings 17:13, 14).

The prophet Elijah made a breathtaking promise on God's behalf. He told the woman that God would ensure she never ran out of supplies. He told her that her one jar of flour and her one jug of oil would last as long as it was needed, until the famine ended and she could feed her son again. But the promise came with a challenge. Elijah still wanted the bread for himself, and he wanted her to give it to him first, before she fed her son and herself.

There are moments in life when God calls us to take a bold, risky step of faith. Very often, that call comes in the form of a genuine need from someone else.

I think that most mothers would draw the line at this point! We're usually willing to help others where we can, but give bread to a stranger when we haven't got enough to feed our own children? Are you kidding?

What was Elijah's problem? Was he being greedy, demanding, or unreasonable? On the surface of the story it certainly looks that way.

But Elijah's encounter with the widow of Zarephath was an acted parable—acted out in the life of this woman who was not an Israelite, but who knew about the God of Israel. The God of heaven promised to provide for her, though she was not one of the Chosen People. But first, He asked her to step out in faith. Did she trust enough to give away her last bit of flour and oil, believing that God would supply more?

It seems incredible, but she did. 1 Kings 17:15 tells us simply, "She went away and did as Elijah had told her." For whatever reason, she trusted this unknown God and His prophet enough to take that step of faith. Maybe she was so desperate she thought it could do no harm to take a risk. When you're only one small flatbread away from starvation, perhaps it's time to throw caution to the winds.

So often, when we're in a difficult situation, we become wary. We close in, reluctant to share the little we have with others. Whether it's money, space, time, or emotions we reason, "I have hardly any left for myself. I can't afford to share."

There are definitely times when it's wise to conserve our resources, but there are also moments in life when God calls us to take a bold, risky step of faith. Very often, that call comes in the form of a genuine need from someone else. God challenges us, "If you respond with generosity to the needs of others, I'll supply your needs. Trust Me. Take a chance."

While collecting door-to-door for a charitable organization in our hometown, my friends and I observed that the best neighborhoods with the biggest homes didn't necessarily result in the best bottom line at the end of the day. Some of the most steady and generous giving came from people in public housing units, people with little change to spare. It seems obvious that those with the most to give would be most generous, but that's not always the way.

It's the difference between living with an attitude of abundance and an attitude of lack. People with a "lack" attitude are always hoarding, always careful, reluctant to give or share. No matter the balance in their bank account, they never think they have enough, so their focus is always on holding tight to what they have. Some of these people can be fabulously wealthy, yet completely unwilling to share what they have with others.

If you live with a mentality of abundance, then you truly believe the Bible promise that "My God will meet all your needs according to his glorious riches in Christ Jesus" (Philippians 4:19). He did it for the widow of Zarephath. Every day she went back and checked her jar of flour and her jug of oil, and each day, miraculously, there was just enough there to make one more loaf of bread for herself, her son, and Elijah. She trusted God enough to feed and care for a stranger when she didn't even have enough for herself, and God rewarded that trust. She had the attitude of abundance that says, "God's grace is enough—and because of it I have enough to share with others."

If you feel you're running out of resources, trust God. He may challenge you to share with someone else. That may be the very path He uses to meet all your needs.

The Slave GIRL

When someone mistreats you, how do you respond?
What if you had to work under that person's supervision every day?
Could you treat them with Christian love?

A young girl in a war-torn country awakes one night to screams. Enemy soldiers have attacked her village. The raid is brutal, bloody, and lightning-swift. Her people are caught off-guard. Before dawn lights the sky, the girl is in chains, being marched away from the only home she's ever known. She leaves behind father, mother, brothers, and sisters. She has no idea if they're alive or dead or if she'll ever see any of them or her home, again.

Fate is kind to her, relatively speaking. For a young girl captured in war and made a slave, there were many fates worse than domestic service in a wealthy home. The girl found herself working in the home of a high-ranking army commander, serving the commander's wife. Life was better than it could have been—except that it would never be the same. Home, family, and everything familiar was gone forever.

What an adjustment that must have been! Today, we would expect someone who'd been through such a terrible experience to suffer from post-traumatic stress disorder, and perhaps she did. But she wasn't the only person in that house suffering. The master of the house, the army commander, suffered from the terrible skin disease known in Bible times as leprosy. There was no known cure, and the condition inevitably led to the sufferer being cast out of society.

I wonder what this slave girl felt when she first learned that Naaman, commander of the army of Aram, was a leper? The natural reaction might be to gloat over the suffering of the man who had caused such suffering to her and her people. She might have reflected with pleasure on the fact that he would someday be outcast and cut off from his people, just as she now was from hers.

On the other hand—if you can't beat 'em, join 'em. Some people might react to such a tragic loss by moving forward and trying to forget the past. The slave girl might have said to herself, "I'm a citizen of Aram now. The God of Israel has forgotten me, so I'll forget Him. I'll assimilate to the culture, try to fit in. I'll even worship the gods of Aram." She might have felt sorry for Naaman, and prayed to the gods of his country to heal him.

But the slave girl did neither. She didn't cling to bitterness and resentment, but neither did she forget who she was and where she came from. Somehow, though she was only a young girl and had suffered the loss of everything dear to her, she managed to be faithful to the God of heaven and still show respect and even love for the man who had taken her away from Israel. Hundreds of years before Jesus told people to love their enemies, she demonstrated a spirit of forgiveness and generosity most Christians wouldn't be able to imitate.

Second Kings 5:3 records what the slave girl said to Naaman's wife upon learning of her master's illness: "She said to her mistress, 'If only my master would see the prophet who is in Samaria! He would cure him of his leprosy.'"

This young girl was able to show kindness and forgiveness to a man who, by every human standard, should have been her enemy. Yet in loving the enemy, she didn't compromise her own standards or beliefs. She wanted Naaman to be cured, and she pointed him towards the prophet of God, Elisha, in her own country.

That slave girl was able to walk a finer line than most of us can manage. When faced with an enemy—someone who has hurt us, someone who attacks everything we stand for—it's so natural to respond with resentment. We want to see them suffer just as they've made us suffer. We delight in their pain. Most of us are a long way from the spirit of Jesus, who said, "Love your enemies and pray for those who persecute you" (Matthew 5:44).

Perhaps we're afraid that if we love and pray for our enemies, we'll fall into the opposite trap. We'll condone their evil deeds, accept their values, maybe allow our standards to slip. It happens. There's a well-known phenomenon known as the "Stockholm syndrome" in which people who are held hostage begin to sympathize with their captures, to identify with the goals and aims of those who have taken them hostage. In a world where God's people are often hostages to sin and evil, we may be in danger of sympathizing with the enemy.

Naaman's slave girl wasn't a victim of Stockholm syndrome. She didn't identify with the people of Aram or their gods. She knew who she was—an Israelite, a servant of the God of heaven. She was generous and kind to her master, not because she was brainwashed into doing so, but because she truly understood the all-encompassing love of God. She had that rare ability to recognize that what another person has done is truly wrong, yet to forgive them and wish the best for them. Forgiving Naaman didn't mean erasing who she was. It meant having the courage to stand up in that foreign place and speak the name of God's prophet, to point her captor towards the God who could heal and forgive him.

It takes more courage to love your enemies, to reach out in genuine kindness to those who have hurt you.

Sometimes we experience conflict with people and we can honestly say "There are two sides to the story. We were both to blame." At other times, there's a very clear right and wrong, and we can see that we and those around us have been the victims of evil. Like the slave girl, we have been hurt and abused by evil people and the evil system they serve.

In that situation it takes courage to go on being who you are, holding to your own values and beliefs. It takes even more courage to love your enemies, to reach out in genuine kindness to those who have hurt you.

Naaman must have respected the young slave girl. Perhaps he saw in her something of what we see as we read her story today. He recognized a unique individual who was capable of speaking with truth and love in a difficult situation. So he listened to her advice, and he did what she suggested. He went to the prophet Elisha, and he was healed of his leprosy.

We never learn the sequel to the story. Naaman returned to his home healed, declaring that he would "never again make burnt offerings and sacrifices to any other god but the Lord" (2 Kings 5:17). The slave girl's one-woman missionary effort had been a success, but as for her fate, we're not told.

It would be nice to believe that as a reward for her good advice, Naaman freed her and returned her to her home. It would be nice to believe that she found her family still alive and enjoyed a joyous reunion with them. Maybe she did. Or perhaps she lived out the rest of her life as a slave in a foreign land, with her strong faith continuing to sustain her. Whatever her destiny, her brief appearance on the pages of Scripture reminds us all of how God calls us to react in difficult times.

ESTHER

Does your life feel like it's spinning out of control?
So did Esther's. But she discovered she still had a choice.

In a remote mountain village, a poor family struggles for subsistence. A big-city stranger spots their pretty 12-year-old daughter and tells the parents he can offer her a better life working at a factory in the city. He assures them she will send money home to help support the family. With tears, kisses, and prayers the parents send their little girl to the city—where the stranger rents her as a prostitute to wealthy businessmen. Her life becomes a nightmare of sexual exploitation, with no hope of escape.

That frightening scenario is reality for many young girls around the world. But what does it have to do with a favorite Bible story about a brave and beautiful queen?

The journey of the Jewish girl, Hadassah, to become the Persian Queen Esther is often pictured as a glamorous ancient beauty pageant, a sort of "Persian Idol," if you like! Taken into the king's harem, she is chosen from among dozens of young girls to become the king's new wife. But in Esther's world, women were property. Powerful men exercised their right to take any woman they wanted, with or without her consent. No one considered whether Esther, a frightened and inexperienced teenager, wanted to be in King Xerxes' harem or not.

Esther's foster father, Mordecai, warned her to keep her Jewish background a secret. Hiding her true identity was just one burden among many Esther would have had to bear. In the harem, she lived in a closeted world of women and eunuchs. To us modern women, the full year of massage and beauty treatments described in the book of Esther may sound like an endless spa weekend. But imagine the boredom, the stagnation, of a place in which dozens, perhaps hundreds of women had no purpose in life except to please a single man. Many of them would see the king only once in their lives. If the king enjoyed a particular girl, she might briefly become a harem favorite—and instantly plunged into a storm of political conflict. And if she didn't please the king, there was no going back home. No hope of marrying and enjoying a family and a household of her own. A harem girl was the king's property forever, trapped in a suffocating cloister rife with rivalry and bereft of purpose.

No matter what your circumstances, you have a choice. Choose to respond creatively, with courage and Christian faithfulness.

That was the life that faced Esther. The Bible gives us no clue what her hopes and dreams might have been before "she was taken to the king's palace" (Esther 2:8). She probably dreamed of marriage and children. Maybe she even hoped to travel to Jerusalem, where other returned Jewish exiles were trying to rebuild a life and a nation. Her hopes and dreams didn't matter. In that society, a woman's own desires counted for very little, and once a king's lust entered the picture, they didn't count at all.

Esther must have wondered, perhaps even pleaded with God: Why did You allow this to happen? What's Your purpose for me? Why was a good Jewish girl fated to become Playmate of the Month for a pagan king? Then five years later, when the Jews of Persia faced genocide, Mordecai challenged the young Queen Esther to go uninvited to the king's throne room to plead for her people—even though appearing before His Majesty without being summoned was a crime punishable by death. When Mordecai tells Esther, "Who knows but that you have come to royal position for such a time as this?" (Esther 4:14), we hear in the background the question Esther must have asked: Why am I here?

A woman need not be a child prostitute in downtown Bangkok to relate to Esther's story. Tragedy, chronic illness, abuse, financial collapse—situations spin out of control, and we find ourselves in places we never would have chosen to be. Like Esther, we cry, "Why have you allowed this to happen to me, Lord? What's your purpose in bringing me here?"

Our life circumstances aren't always the ones we would choose. Indeed, those circumstances don't always reflect God's perfect will for us. Another beloved Old Testament story, the book of Job, allows us a behind-the-scenes glimpse at how God's sovereignty interacts with the reality of a fallen world. Satan asks God for permission to test Job's loyalty by taking away his wealth, health, and family—yet Job remains loyal. God's perfect will for His followers is happiness, health, and wholeness. But against the backdrop of the Great Controversy between God and the forces of evil, God allows suffering so that both He and His people can be vindicated in the eyes of the watching universe. God allowed Satan to derail the perfect life He had planned for Job. And God relied on Job to make the choices that would allow God's will to ultimately prevail (see Job 1 and 2).

Maybe God's perfect will for Esther would have been marriage to a good Jewish man, and a return to Jerusalem. The Bible doesn't speculate. But in a fallen world God's will proves big enough to encompass even the selfish lust of a Persian tyrant—as long as Esther cooperates. As long as this frightened Jewish teenage girl can exercise the one power that remains to her: the power to make a choice.

When circumstances fly out of control, we feel powerless, frightened, alone, and abused. But we always have a choice. Esther couldn't choose to stay out of the harem. She couldn't choose to skip her appointment with the king. But she could choose how to respond. She could choose courage. She could choose faithfulness. She chose to risk her life by pleading for her people—bravely defying the king's authority with the words, "If I perish, I perish" (Esther 4:16). Because of that choice, her name rings through history as an example of courageous, God-fearing womanhood.

When you look around at turbulent, painful circumstances; when you look up at an empty sky and cry, "God—why? Why am I here?" remember Esther. You have a choice. You can choose how to respond. That choice may involve changing the circumstances, such as when a woman is called to leave an abusive relationship. Or it may involve staying and transforming difficult circumstances, such as the woman who cares for a disabled family member with grace and compassion. When you make the choice that honors God, you become His co-worker.

This amazes me—that the sovereign God of the universe allows teenage sex slaves and abused housewives and stressed-out single moms and chronically ill senior citizens to become His partners. He says to us, "I have a plan for your life. But this is a sinful world, and I value free will. I won't pull all the strings. I rely on you to make a choice, so that my will can be done on earth as it is in heaven." We can choose to do things God's way, even in difficult situations.

No matter what your circumstances, you have a choice. Make Esther's choice. Choose to respond creatively, with courage and Christian faithfulness. You, too, may go down in history as one of God's heroines.

Mary
of NAZARETH

Ever feel like you've given up your whole life for your family or others whom you care for?
You're not the first woman to feel that way.

A teenage girl, pregnant before her marriage. Hardly an unusual situation today. A little more unusual in her day, but still not unheard-of.

Eyebrows were raised. Gossips whispered. The old women shook their heads, walking back from the well with their water jars in the morning sunshine. "Such a quiet girl . . . such a good family . . . who'd ever have thought it?"

Mary walked alone, a little apart from the others. Indeed, who would have thought it? And who will believe me? she wondered. Would her parents? Her friends? Would Joseph, her fiance? If anyone should trust her, it should be Joseph. But he was the least likely to trust her now. And how could anyone believe such an incredible story?

Probably no woman in the Bible is better known or more talked-about than Mary of Nazareth, the young girl called to be the mother of Jesus. Yet despite all the stories, the songs, the paintings, and sculpture she remains a mystery to us. The words of the angel's announcement are familiar to us now: "Rejoice, highly favored one, the Lord is with you; blessed are you among women!" (Luke 1:28, NKJV). But to Mary's ears, the words did not have the familiar ring of an old, comforting song. Those words were a shocking jolt, jarring her out of a familiar and predictable life into a life of radical obedience and total commitment.

The highlights of her story are well-known. Pregnant out of wedlock and with no good story to explain the situation, she risked rejection by her fiancé—until another angel intervened. Uprooted from her home, without her mother or familiar midwife to attend her, Mary gave birth in a barn and placed her newborn in a feed trough. Then, hunted by Roman soldiers, her family fled the country, becoming refugees and living among strangers.

How she loved the Son whose birth had caused so much difficulty! Yet He never stopped giving her trouble. No doubt He was obedient and dutiful: the Bible tells us that Jesus "went down to Nazareth with [Mary and Joseph] and was obedient to them" (Luke 2:51). But His obedience was that of a strong-willed Child who knew that He had a calling and a mission that would eventually upset His family. A later glimpse of Mary shows her with her other, less troublesome sons, trying to convince Him that He should give up this Messiah business and come home (see Mark 3:20, 21, 31-34). There, as on other occasions, Jesus makes His priorities clear: His ministry came ahead of His commitment to family, even to His own mother.

She must have known what kind of Son He'd be. She must have known—when He was 12 years old and became so engaged in discussing the Law with the rabbis at the Temple that He completely missed the call to pack up and go home, and then coolly told His parents He was doing His heavenly Father's business (Luke 2:49). Even earlier, at His dedication ceremony, a prophet in the Temple foretold Jesus' future greatness with the cryptic warning to Mary, "A sword will pierce your own soul too" (Luke 2:35).

That sword never stopped piercing Mary's soul. It made the first cut the day she had to tell her parents and her fiancé that she was inexplicably pregnant. And as Jesus grew and discovered His mission and moved steadily further away from the circle of home and safety, the sword continued to slice Mary's heart. Finally it plunged in to the hilt as she stood at the foot of His cross. Her troublesome boy, her strong-willed child, had gotten Himself into trouble for the last time. His reckless words had finally stirred the anger of the authorities, and He hung above her head, dying a slow, terrible public death from suffocation.

For this Son she had given up the normal life she might have had. She had become an object of gossip and suspicion. She had given up peace of mind and security, living on the edge of fear as public opinion turned against Jesus. Did she guess, when the angel said, "Blessed are you among women!" that the sword's cut would be so deep, and so final?

Do any of us guess? For most of us God's call to obedience doesn't come in the form of an angelic messenger. Rather, His call is simpler, couched in the form of a choice we make. We marry. We have a child. We form a friendship. We know, in a vague sense, that God demands we do our very best in these relationships. We know that we will be called to give sacrificially, but we hardly imagine the level of commitment He will ask of us.

Having a child is a life-changing event. Jesus gave His life for the world; Mary, in some senses, gave up her life for Jesus. But every good mother sacrifices her life for her child—sacrifices the selfish pleasures of sleeping late in the morning and going out with her friends every evening, sacrifices a portion of her own goals and dreams to invest time and energy in helping her child grow into adulthood. Every parent knows a little of Mary's pain; the point of that sword has touched all our souls.

The sword's touch is not limited to the hearts of mothers. Everyone who has truly loved another person—their child, a spouse, a parent, a friend, a student, a patient—knows the commitment that call requires, and the pain that love can bring. The call to love is a dangerous call, one to which we respond at our peril. But it's a call God extends to each one of us. We are invited to take the risk of loving, knowing that it will mean pain and sacrifice. If we can respond, as Mary did—"I am the Lord's servant. . . . May it be to me as you have said"—then we will hear, as she did, God's blessing: "Do not be afraid . . . you have found favor with God."

The weeping mother at the foot of the cross is not our final glimpse of Mary. We see her before dawn on Sunday morning, hurrying down to her Son's tomb to pay a final tribute. Like the other women, she finds an empty tomb and hears the message of a risen Jesus.

We learn how Jesus' good friend and follower Mary Magdalene responded to that news. We hear how His disciples Peter and John reacted. We even learn of the responses of doubting Thomas and couple of nameless extras on the road to Emmaus. But none of the Gospel writers shows us a meeting between the risen Jesus and His mother. No one bothers to record how Mary felt when she found that her unpredictable, headstrong Son had done the most unpredictable thing of all—burst out His tomb and defeated death for all eternity.

Maybe we don't need to know. Any mother can imagine. Any woman who has loved knows what Mary knew: the sacrifice is real; the pain is real. But they are nothing compared to the reward.

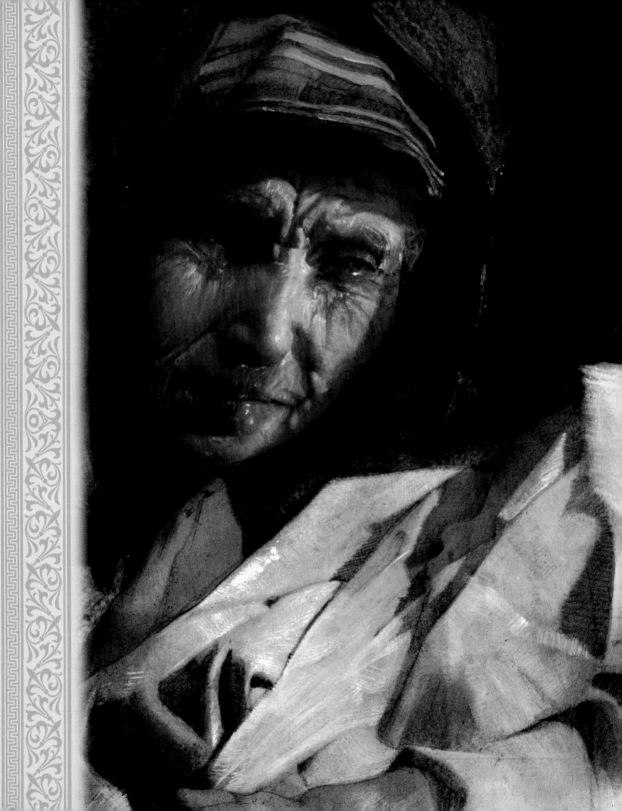

ANNA

Have you ever felt that it's too late?
Anna, the prophet, might encourage you not to give up hope.

She sat in her usual spot in the outer court of the Temple, watching and waiting. She had watched and waited for so long now that she often thought she might lose hope. Surely she would die before the hope she'd cherished for so long was fulfilled. Day after day she sat in this same spot, praying and often fasting, waiting for the Lord to send her another message, to finish what He'd started so long ago. And every night for many years she lay down to rest on her lonely pillow, still waiting.

But today was different. Today her old eyes spotted a young man and woman coming into the Temple carrying a baby. Not, in itself, an unusual sight. But something about the threesome made her heart beat faster. "Is this it, Lord?" she asked quietly.

Anna was an old woman—at least 84 years of age, if not older. (Bible translations aren't clear on whether she was an 84-year-old widow or whether she'd been a widow for 84 years. Either way, she was an elderly woman.)

She is introduced to us briefly in Luke 2:36, 37: "There was also a prophetess, Anna, the daughter of Phanuel, of the tribe of Asher. She was very old; she had lived with her husband seven years after her marriage, and then was a widow until she was eighty-four. She never left the temple but worshiped night and day, fasting and praying."

Anna's life had started out in a predictable way—she was married, probably very young, and began fulfilling the roles society expected of a woman. But after only seven years of marriage, her husband died. Rather than marrying again, as everyone might have expected—and as, perhaps, her family encouraged her to do—Anna was led down a different path. The Bible calls her a "prophetess"—someone who receives a message from God.

We don't know exactly what God's message to Anna was, but since she is featured in Luke's gospel as part of the story of the baby Jesus' dedication at the Temple, we can assume that, like the other aging prophet in that story, Simeon (Luke 2:25-35), she had been given a vision or message about the coming Deliverer, the Messiah who would redeem Israel.

After receiving a word from God, Anna's life had been changed. No longer did she stay on the safe and predictable path. Instead, she moved into the Temple and dedicated her life to God, spending all her time in worship, fasting, and prayer—a very unusual decision, especially for a woman.

Family and friends must have questioned whether Anna was going crazy, whether she was taking her devotion to God a little too far. "Serving the Lord is all very well," some might have cautioned, "but you need some balance in your life. You don't need to *move* in to the Temple—just visit now and then! And is all this fasting really good for your health?"

Her old eyes spotted a young man and woman coming into the Temple carrying a baby. Something about them made her heart beat faster. "Is this it, Lord?" she asked quietly.

But Anna must have been confident in the call she had received from God. She was going to live the life He had called her to, unconventional though it was.

If God gave you a call to do something really unusual, to defy tradition and good advice and strike out in faith, wouldn't you expect confirmation—quickly—that you were on the right path? Wouldn't you hope He would do something impressive to justify your faithful obedience?

That's what most of us would hope for. We may be willing to take a step of faith, but we want to make sure there's solid ground under our feet. We may take a risk for God, but we want to see results quickly—evidence that He's blessing us. And if we don't, discouragement may swiftly follow.

Anna didn't get instant gratification after her bold step of faith. She waited for years—for decades—until that morning when Mary and Joseph brought the infant Jesus to the Temple to be dedicated. She was old, probably tired and near death, when she finally saw and recognized the fulfillment of the vision God had given her so long ago.

Luke 2:38 tells us what she did when the moment finally arrived: "Coming up to them at that very moment, she gave thanks to God and spoke about the child to all who were looking forward to the redemption of Jerusalem."

The Bible doesn't record Anna's words for us as it does Simeon's, but it does tell us that she spoke about the baby Jesus to people—the people who were waiting for a Redeemer, expecting a Messiah. She told people that this obscure Baby born of poor Galilean parents was the One they had been waiting for. Maybe people didn't believe her. Perhaps only a few listened. But it doesn't seem to have mattered to Anna. She had seen what she'd waited so many years for. Her long vigil had finally ended.

> *Anna didn't get instant gratification after her bold step of faith. She was old, probably tired and near death, when she finally saw and recognized the fulfillment of the vision God had given her so long ago.*

Do you get discouraged when you don't see results? When you try to serve God faithfully, yet feel that He hasn't responded? Perhaps you've been involved in ministry, taken a step of faith to serve Him, yet not seen the success you'd hoped for. Perhaps you've been praying for years for children or other loved ones to come to the Lord, and feel that your prayers go unheard. Perhaps you've given up a great deal—security, career, even love—to follow the Lord, and feel that He hasn't come through with the rewards you expected.

And maybe the years are rushing by, just as they did for Anna. Some older women may look back on their lives and ask, "What did I accomplish? Did I do the things God wanted me to do? Were my sacrifices, my efforts, worth it all?" If the answer seems to be "No," some may feel it's too late. Once you've reached retirement age, society decides you've passed your expiry date. How can anything rewarding, anything important, happen to you after your hair is gray?

That's the prejudice of our youth-obsessed society—but Anna would laugh at it. She knew that 84 wasn't too old for God to do something exciting for her. She knew that years of faithfulness *would* be rewarded. Indeed, Anna's long vigil in the Temple was its own reward, for she spent that time in the presence of God, learning to love Him and worship Him.

> *Can anything rewarding, anything important, happen to you after your hair is gray? Anna knew that 84 wasn't too old for God to do something exciting for her. She knew that years of faithfulness would be rewarded.*

Yes, she was waiting—but not waiting in discouragement, not waiting without hope. She was waiting with the secure knowledge that God would fulfill His promises—and that it would never be too late.

If you've ever felt that it was "too late" for God to work in your life, take heart! He's there. He's working, even if His efforts take place quietly behind the scenes. If, like Anna, you learn to live in His presence and love it, you'll know it's never too late.

The Woman at the WELL

Do you ever feel like your life is in a dead-end pattern?
Do you keep repeating the same mistakes over and over?
Meet a woman who knew exactly how that felt—
but who took the risk of trying something completely different.

On a hot, dry, dusty noonday a woman comes alone to the village well to draw water. Most women came to the well in the cool morning hours, but she didn't want to be there when "most women" were. She knew what it felt like to be on the receiving end of gossipy whispers and suspicious stares. She preferred to avoid company and avoid trouble.

Trouble had followed her all her life. The Bible doesn't tell us her name or her age. In fact, we know only one important thing about her biography, and that is that she had been married five times and was now living with a man not her husband (see John 4:18).

Today, the phrase "married five times" probably calls up images of a Hollywood star who breezes through one short-term marriage after another, discarding husbands like old clothing. But to place the story of this biblical woman in context, we need to remember that in ancient cultures, women never initiated divorce. A marriage ended only with the death of one partner or when a husband rejected or abandoned his wife.

We don't know what string of tragedies had led this woman through five marriages. Was she a widow five times over? Perhaps she was unable to bear a child—a situation which might have led one husband after another to reject her. Perhaps she repeatedly strayed outside of her marriages, causing her husbands to rid themselves of her. Or perhaps it was a combination of bad luck and bad conduct on both sides. The one thing we know for sure is that after five unsuccessful trips to the altar, her value in that society was nonexistent. As a widow or a rejected wife, she was completely without worth. In fact, she was held in such low esteem that a man was openly living with her without marrying her—in her society, the ultimate disgrace.

For years, her life had been trapped in a pattern from which there seemed no escape. Each new marriage had probably been greeted with hope and optimism. Perhaps this time she would be happily married, have a family, and find success and worth in the eyes of those around her. But time after time, each marriage failed. Each time she found herself alone, a little less valuable, a little less worthy in the eyes of the community—and in her own eyes.

Left to herself, this woman had no idea how to break the cycle. By living with a man outside marriage, she was taking the only option left available to her. By now no one else would marry her, yet she knew no other path to self-worth and social acceptance than to depend on a man. As she trudged to the well in the hot midday sun, this nameless Samaritan woman had reached the limits of her hope, her faith, and her courage.

Usually, the well was unoccupied in the middle of the day. But today, she found something different. She found a man sitting by the well.

He was unfamiliar. In fact, she recognized that he was not a Samaritan at all, but a Jew. She knew that he would have nothing but contempt for her—both because she was a woman, and because of her race. If he knew about her unhappy history, he would have even less reason to tolerate her.

But that was of little consequence. Men didn't address strange women they ran into on the streets. It was unacceptable behavior. Averting her eyes, she had begun lowering her bucket into the well when she was surprised by the most unexpected conversation of her life.

Seemingly out of nowhere, Jesus said, "Will you give me a drink?"

She was shocked. "You are a Jew and I am a Samaritan woman. How can you ask me for a drink?" she gasped.

"Jesus answered her, 'If you knew the gift of God and who it is that asks you for a drink, you would have asked him and he would have given you living water'" (John 4:10).

In a life that has fallen into a routine of failure, something completely unexpected breaks through—the Son of God, sitting by a village well without a bucket or a cup. In Jesus' simple human need for a drink, He reaches out to this woman and touches her far greater need—her need for a life of meaning and value.

The Samaritan woman responded to Jesus' surprising approach. She was intrigued by His idea of "living water," although it took her awhile to realize that he was talking not about something to drink but about an inner spiritual renewal that could transform her life.

The life-changing moment in the conversation came when Jesus asked her to go call her husband. When she replied that she had no husband, Jesus used His prophetic insight to reveal the shame of her past and present life. He knew all about it. But in spite of all that, Jesus considered her worth talking to. He saw her as someone whose life could be transformed by God's gift of living water. And because Jesus saw her with new eyes, this woman's life was changed forever.

The same woman who shamefully crept to the well at noon to avoid hostile looks and cutting words, now ran back to the village, shouting her story at the top of her lungs. No longer was she afraid to attract attention. Her life no longer centered around her own failure, but around the hope Jesus offered.

"Then, leaving her water jar, the woman went back to the town and said to the people, 'Come, see a man who told me everything I ever did. Could this be the Christ?'" (John 4:28).

The Samaritan woman left more than her water jar at that well. She left her sense of inferiority, her identity as a failed wife and an immoral woman. She walked away focused not on herself, but on Jesus. In opening herself to an unexpected conversation, she had found the way to break out of a cycle of failure and despair.

If your life seems to be caught in a dead-end cycle, if you feel that your value and self-worth has been lost somewhere along the way, Jesus offers hope. He reaches out in unexpected ways—through a simple conversation, an opportunity to help someone else, a moment alone in prayer—and gives you the promise of something better.

The living water that He offered to the Samaritan woman is available to you and me today. All we need to do is lay down our water jars—along with our failures, our despair, our lack of self-worth—and open ourselves up to the unexpected. Open up to Jesus and all that He has to give.

The Canaanite WOMAN

If God says no to your prayers, does it mean He doesn't care?

Nobody knows heartache and despair like the mother of a sick child. If you've been there, you know the sheer agony that comes from watching your helpless child in pain, knowing you'd do anything to spare her but realizing how powerless you are. Most mothers, faced with that particular challenge, would reach out for virtually anyone or anything that promised help.

A woman who lived 2,000 years ago, a woman whose name no one bothered to record, experienced that timeless anguish. She lived on the edges of the Jewish nation, in "the region of Tyre and Sidon." But she wasn't Jewish; she was Canaanite. She had no particular reason to worship or be interested in the God of Israel or in any preacher or prophet who taught about that God. She was an outsider, an alien. She knew that the Jews looked down on her as a Gentile, someone not worthy of respect in their world. Some would even consider her less than human. But until her daughter became ill, that probably didn't matter much to her.

Then, quite suddenly, it did matter. Because she heard of a man who was passing through the area, a Jewish rabbi, a teacher and preacher, who had gained quite a reputation. Once again, she had no particular reason to be interested in Jewish teachers or preachers. Why should she put herself in the way of someone who was only going to look down on her or despise her?

But then she heard that this travelling preacher, this Jesus of Nazareth, was something more than just a rabbi. He was best known as a miracle-worker, a healer so powerful that people believed His power came directly from God. He had given sight to the blind, made lame people walk, cured lepers—and cast out demons. The Canaanite woman's beloved daughter was demon-possessed.

She probably knew little about the Jewish religion and nothing about the Hebrew Scriptures or the prophecies. She had no opinions about a coming Messiah or about what it meant to be the Son of God. She was interested in Jesus of Nazareth for one reason and one only: He was a healer. He could cast out demons. So she sought Him out and threw herself at His feet, begging Him to heal her daughter.

Here's where the story becomes very strange. Jesus ignored her. Jesus, who was always quick to respond to anyone in need of help or healing, simply didn't answer the woman at all. Read it in Matthew 15: 23: "Jesus did not answer a word. So his disciples came to him and urged him, 'Send her away, for she keeps crying out after us.'"

Jesus' response is puzzling in view of how He normally treated people, but it may make sense to parents who have faced the frightening reality of a child's illness. Crying out to God for help is a natural thing to do, but how often do we seem to be met with a deafening silence? Many people can testify that when life is at a crisis, when things seem to be most terrifying, they cry out to God and receive only empty silence for an answer. Sometimes, it seems that God ignores us.

Some people might become bitter or resentful at such a response. But not this Canaanite woman. The only that mattered to her was her daughter. So she tried again.

This time she got a response. But it wasn't the encouraging, faith-building response she had hoped for. Instead, Jesus said to her, "'It is not right to take the children's bread and toss it to their dogs'" (Matthew 15:26).

At this point, the woman must have thought she finally understood. It was about racial and religious prejudice, after all. The Jews were God's chosen people, the children of God. On the other hand, Gentiles such as herself, were no better than the mongrel dogs that slunk around the streets. At those harsh words from Jesus' own mouth you might imagine the woman just shrinking into herself, giving up, going home in despair.

But that's not what she did. Instead, she talked back to Jesus. A Gentile woman talking back to a respected Jewish rabbi! According to every social norm of her time, she was way out of line. According to our understanding of who Jesus was, she was actually talking back to God! But once again, nothing mattered to her except finding the help and healing she needed for the daughter she so dearly loved.

Her comeback was as snappy as anything a Hollywood comedy writer could have come up with: "'Yes, Lord,' she said, 'but even the dogs eat the crumbs that fall from their masters' table'" (Matthew 15:27).

When you knock on God's door with all your strength and get no answer—don't give up. He's listening. He's waiting. And yes, He does care.

It's hard not to hear a hint of laughter in Jesus' voice as He replies, "'Woman, you have great faith! Your request is granted'" (vs. 28). And, the Bible tells us that her daughter was healed from that very moment.

And so, the story has a happy ending. The Canaanite woman goes home, and her daughter is healed. Jesus rewards her for the faith that enables her to be persistent even in the face of His own discouraging response.

But the Bible reader is left with a huge "Why"? The Canaanite woman wasn't shocked by Jesus' response. She expected no better from a Jewish rabbi, and was probably thrilled that He even listened to her, much less healed her daughter. But as Christians we know that Jesus was more than an ordinary man of His times, with the usual prejudices. We know that Jesus was the Son of God, that He showed infinite love and compassion to every human being—including people who weren't Jewish. So why did He respond in such an uncharacteristic way to this woman who only wanted healing for her child?

The Bible doesn't tell us. Jesus' actions aren't explained. Placing them in context with the rest of His actions and attitudes, our best guess might be that His response was a parody of the way His disciples felt about Gentiles. We sense that Jesus acted out their own prejudices in order to teach them a lesson.

But the fact is that we often don't understand why God doesn't respond to our prayers, our pleas for help. His motives, like Jesus' motives in this encounter, often aren't clear to us in the here-and-now of our everyday lives. Sometimes we throw ourselves at His feet, we beg and plead for help in the most painful situations in our lives, and we're met with only silence—or worse, with what seems like rejection.

What do we do then? Do we give up in despair, or bow our heads in submission and say, "I guess my problems are too insignificant for God to worry about"?

Jesus liked persistence. He liked people like the Canannite woman, whose faith was strong enough that they didn't give up. When you knock on God's door with all your strength and get no answer—don't give up. You may not understand the reasons for His silence, but He's still there. He's listening. He's waiting. And yes, He does care.

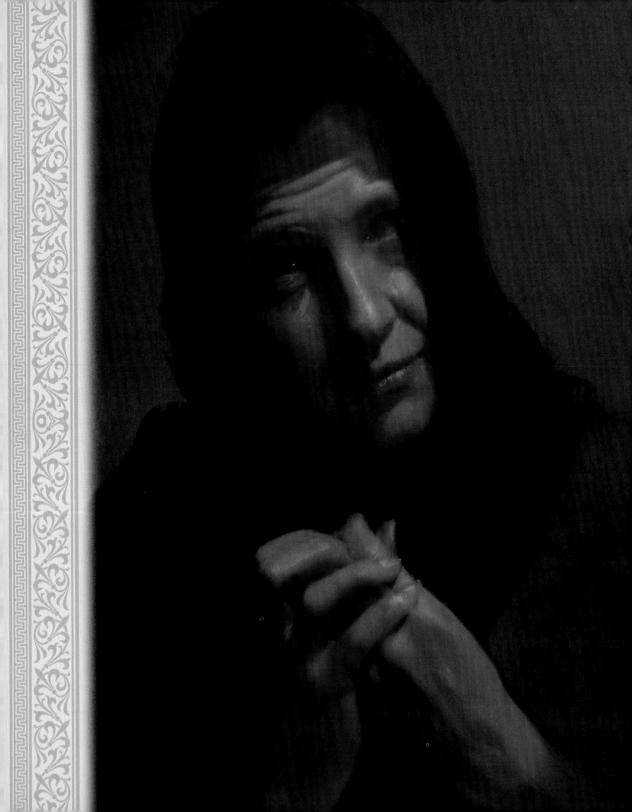

The Widow of NAIN

She lost everything when her son died.
It seemed her life was at an end. Then Jesus said to her, "Don't cry."

The funeral procession wound its sad, slow way out through the town gates toward the burial place. At the head of the procession was the grieving mother of the deceased—not riding in a hearse, but walking on foot behind the pallet which bore the covered body of her only son. Behind her, relatives, friends, neighbors, and hired mourners filled the air with their loud wails. But the dead boy's mother was silent. Her grief was too intense to be shouted to the skies. It was locked in her heart, a heart that she was sure would never feel light or happy again.

She was mourning as any mother would mourn the loss of her child—a young man whose life was cut short in the prime of his youth, without a chance to grow to full manhood.

But there was another layer to her grief. In her culture, a woman without a man to care for her was destitute. This woman was a widow. No doubt she had lived in poverty for years, waiting for the day when her only son would be able to take up his father's trade and support them both. But that day had barely come when her boy was taken from her.

She lost not only a beloved child, but any hope of a livelihood and security for her old age.

No wonder she walked at the head of the funeral procession, her head cast down, talking to no one, seeing nothing. Her world had ended. She couldn't see past the loss that had swallowed her past, present, and future.

Looking at the ground, she didn't see the other, smaller, procession approaching the gates of Nain even as they were leaving.

It wasn't a formal procession like the funeral. Rather, it was a popular preacher and healer named Jesus of Nazareth, accompanied by His friends, His disciples, and the curious crowd of onlookers that seemed to follow Him wherever He went. They knew that if they stayed close to Jesus they would hear life-changing truths and see miracles first-hand. But no one in either procession was prepared for what they were just about to see.

She was the first to see him stir— just a breath that moved the cloth covering his face—and she cried out.

The two processions met right outside the city gates. The woman at the head of one procession looked up, at last, to see the Man at the head of the other.

She didn't know Jesus. She probably hadn't even heard of Him, or if she had, she might have shrugged the stories off. What did a preacher, a healer, a would-be Messiah have to do with her life?

But for her, an encounter with Jesus was about to change absolutely everything.

"When the Lord saw her, his heart went out to her and he said, 'Don't cry.' Then he went up and touched the coffin, and those carrying it stood still. He said, 'Young man, I say to you, get up!'" (Luke 7:13, 14).

The widow looked into the man's eyes as He spoke. He was crazy! Who stopped a funeral procession and told a dead man to get up! But almost against her will, her gaze was torn from the face of Jesus to the covered face of her son's still body lying on the funeral bier.

She was the first to see him stir—just a breath that moved the cloth covering his face—and she cried out. Her cry galvanized the tense crowd, and someone reached to pull the away the cloth. His eyelids fluttered, and he looked up—first into Jesus' face, and then into his mother's.

Can you imagine that woman's joy, her ecstasy at that moment? If you've ever lost a loved one, then of course you can imagine what she felt. Psychologists tell us that for most people the first reaction to grief is denial. We want to turn back time, to deny the reality of the loss, to make it never have happened. At a funeral, the dearest wish of most of the mourners is to have the corpse sit up, look around, and laugh, suddenly well again. We want death itself to be reversed.

The widow from Nain was one of the few people in history who actually had that wish granted. She walked out of the city that day attending her son's body on the way to its burial. She returned hand in hand with her strong, healthy son, rejoicing in God's amazing grace.

It's true that since the time Jesus lived on earth, we no longer see miracles of this nature on an everyday basis. In fact, even during Jesus' 33 years among humanity, we only have record of three times when He brought someone back from death itself. Even for the Son of God, such a miracle was not something to be granted lightly. But those three miracles—one of which was granted to the widow from Nain and her son—are a promise. They are a foretaste, a reminder, of what our God is capable of.

If you've lost someone dear to you, you know what it's like to walk behind a coffin or ride in a hearse wishing that death had never happened, that tragedy could be erased. Yes, we may call that denial, and we do have to accept the reality that in this lifetime, our loved one is gone and won't be coming back.

But in another, deeper sense, our "denial" in the face of death is really a reflection of our deepest hope, our firmest faith. We deny the reality of death because we know death isn't God's ultimate plan for us. We know that Jesus destroyed and defeated death's power over us and that someday He will give us back everything death has taken from us.

The widow of Nain got her son back—for a few years of earthly life. The Bible doesn't say what happened to him, but we can guess that he grew up to care for his mother in her old age, perhaps that he married and presented her with grandchildren to brighten her last years. But of course, one day, perhaps after his mother had been laid to rest, the son, too, died. The people Jesus miraculously restored to life during His earthly ministry lived only to die again a few years later. They were still human, still subject to death's dominion.

But the Bible promises that death isn't the ultimate reality. When we find ourselves wishing death would never happen, we aren't in denial. We're living in hope and faith—the faith that led the apostle Paul to declare: "When the perishable has been clothed with the imperishable, and the mortal with immortality, then the saying that is written will come true: 'Death has been swallowed up in victory.'

Where, O death, is your victory? Where, O death, is your sting?" (1 Corinthians 15:54, 55).

If you, like the widow from Nain, are grieving today for someone you've loved and lost, take hope from Jesus' example and Paul's words. Death will be swallowed up in victory. Death itself will die, defeated by Jesus. When He returns to raise our beloved dead, they will never again feel the sting of the grave. A time is coming when no mother will ever cry over the grave of her child—because all tears will be wiped away forever.

Mary of BETHANY

❧

*Does the idea of making a fool of yourself hold you back
from doing the things God calls you to do?
The woman who used her own hair for a towel might have some advice for you.*

Regional expressions are often full of local color, and the place where I live—Newfoundland—is famous for them. In fact, there's an entire Dictionary of Newfoundland English dedicated to cataloguing some of the more colorful local expressions.

One of my personal favorites is one that we use when a person does something embarrassing in public. Perhaps it's not unique to Newfoundland, but I haven't heard it in other places. Someone who has drawn attention to herself in the most inappropriate way is said to have "made a holy show of herself." I heard this expression a lot as a child and teenager, most often embedded in the sentence, "Don't be making a holy show of yourself!" To make a holy show of yourself was to draw everyone's attention to the fact that you had acted outside the bounds of what was normal, acceptable, and appropriate.

It's this phrase that springs to mind whenever I hear the biblical story of the woman who washed Jesus' feet with her hair. She definitely made a show of herself. A woman with a sinful past, throwing herself before the bare feet of a respectable religious teacher, kissing and crying as she poured perfume all over those feet, and then wiping them dry with her long, uncovered, unbound hair! Shocking. Shameful. Inappropriate. Those words were on the lips of all the guests at that elegant dinner.

But Jesus leapt to her defense. He pointed out that she hadn't just made a show of herself. She had made, in the most literal sense, a holy show of herself. She embarrassed herself for the holiest of reasons—love and gratitude. She stepped outside the bounds of acceptable behavior because she was flamboyantly devoted to Jesus.

The Bible tells this story in different ways, in different places. In Luke 7:36-50 the woman is nameless, but we know she's sinful. Jesus' host points out that fact. The man is shocked that Jesus would allow a sinful woman to touch him so intimately. And Jesus interprets her generous act as a sign of gratitude for the sins He has forgiven.

What Mary proclaimed to the world was that she loved him extravagantly—she didn't care what people thought. She didn't care about her past reputation or the way others might interpret her actions.

In John 12:1-10, the woman is identified as Mary of Bethany, sister of Martha and Lazarus. Jesus has just raised her brother from the dead, and she's naturally grateful, but one of Jesus' disciples makes a fuss about the money wasted on the expensive perfume. Jesus responds that her loving gesture is a preparation for His soon-coming death and burial. Matthew 26 and Mark 14 tell a story very similar to John's, but leave out Mary's name.

Each of the stories centers around the same core moment: the expensive perfume poured on the feet of Jesus and the woman's impulsive, shocking gesture of wiping them with her hair. Since it's unlikely this happened more than once during Jesus' ministry, we must assume that each account tells part of the story, and that the woman was indeed Mary of Bethany, grateful to Jesus not just for her brother's miraculous resurrection, but also for the change Jesus brought into her own life.

The Bible tells us that she was a sinful woman, but not the nature of her sin. Given the expectations of women's behavior at the time, it's often assumed that her sin was sexual in nature, that she was an adulteress, a prostitute, a loose woman. Whatever she had done, it had earned her a reputation. Here was a woman who had already stepped outside the bounds of what society considered normal and acceptable—for the sake of sin.

But then Jesus came and changed everything. With her heart renewed, her family restored, her priorities rearranged, Mary needed to express her gratitude. A quiet "thank you" wouldn't be enough. She wanted to shout her love for Jesus from the rooftops. She wanted everyone to know. She wanted to go just as far outside propriety for the sake of Jesus, as she'd once gone for the sake of the devil.

When Jesus sat down at the Pharisee's table that night, Mary crept into the room, breaking every social taboo in the book. Women were not normally welcome as guests at such gatherings. John 12:2 tells us that Mary's better-behaved sister, Martha, helped serve the guests, which was an appropriate role for a woman.

Jesus' disciples and Martha had been shocked on another occasion—when Mary sat at Jesus' feet listening to Him teach, making herself the equivalent of a male disciple (Luke 10:38-42). Now she went even farther.

Kneeling at Jesus' dusty feet, she poured a bottle of costly perfume over them. Washing a man's feet was the act of a servant, but no servant would burst into tears and kiss the master's feet. That act suggested intimacy, a relationship between lovers. What Mary proclaimed to the world was not that she was Jesus' lover, but that she loved him extravagantly—not as a woman loves a man, but as a child of God loves her Creator and Redeemer. She didn't care what people thought. She didn't care about her past reputation or the way others might interpret her actions.

Letting down her hair was the last straw. Only a loose woman went around with her hair uncovered and unbound. Mary not only showed her hair, but used it as a towel to wipe the perfume and tears from Jesus' feet. How inappropriate! How embarrassing! No wonder people averted their eyes and murmured under their breath as this shameless woman made a holy show of herself.

How often have you been held back from declaring your love for Jesus by fear of what others might think? It might be something small, like going to the front of the church to respond to an altar call. Your heart is touched by the message; you want to respond, but a voice in your head warns, People will think you're fanatical. People will think you've committed some terrible sin. People will stare . . . you'll make a holy show of yourself. And shame—the fear of other people's opinions—keeps you glued to your seat.

Maybe it's something bigger. You have the chance to take a risky step of faith, perhaps pioneering a new ministry that will serve God and others. But the voice of shame speaks up again: What if you fail? What if others disapprove? Will anyone respect you again? Do you really want to make a holy show of yourself?

The next time God calls, don't listen to the little voice of shame. Listen instead to His call, and think of Mary. Think of her overwhelming love for Jesus, her broken bottle of perfume, her uncovered, shameless hair. And remember what Jesus said about Mary: "I tell you the truth, wherever the gospel is preached throughout the world, what she has done will also be told, in memory of her" (Mark 14:9).

And it has been. Because when a woman responds to God's call rather than to the voices of shame and disapproval—when a woman makes a holy show of herself—people notice.

MARTHA

If you seem to be the only one doing the work,
take heart—and a lesson—from Martha.

The house was full of visitors. Outside in the courtyard, the men gathered around Jesus, the teacher, listening to His stories and discussing and sometimes arguing questions of Law and Scripture. In the kitchen, the women's domain, one woman worked alone to prepare a meal for this group of chattering male visitors.

Martha chopped and stirred, sliced and swept, inner resentment seething all the while. Her anger centered on her sister, Mary, the one woman who sat out in the courtyard among the men. She was listening to Jesus, learning from Him as if she were one of His male disciples.

Her place is in here, Martha thought, *helping me! Why am I left to do all the work by myself?*

Finally she could take it no longer. There was just too much work and too few hands to do it! Frustrated, she went out to speak to Jesus.

"Martha was distracted by all the preparations that had to be made. She came to him and asked, 'Lord, don't you care that my sister has left me to do the work by myself? Tell her to help me!'" (Luke 10:40).

No doubt Martha hoped that Jesus would respond with a little sympathy, some appreciation for her hard work, and an order to Mary to go back to the kitchen where she belonged. But instead, Jesus' gentle rebuke was directed not at the sister who sat at His feet, but at the hardworking one who was putting His meal on the table.

Martha, Martha,' the Lord answered, 'you are worried and upset about many things, but only one thing is needed. Mary has chosen what is better, and it will not be taken away from her'" (Luke 10:41, 42).

I'm willing to bet that a lot of women reading this story feel that Martha got a bad deal. After all, it's all very well to sit around and talk about religion and philosophy, but someone has to cook the meals and clean the house! Martha was "worried and upset" about the very things that concern many of us—not just cooking and housework, but caring for others, making sure the needs of our family, friends, and guests are met. Doing what has to get done. What we need is thanks, appreciation, and a little help—not a rebuke.

"Nobody appreciates me! Why aren't they in here helping out?"

Jesus' words might make it sound as though He was placing little value on Martha's diligent efforts and rewarding Mary for doing nothing. But in fact, by praising Mary, Jesus was elevating a woman's status beyond what was usual for the time. He was pointing out that Mary—and Martha, too, if she chose—had just as much right to listen to His teaching and talk with Him as the men did, even though in their society men's and women's roles were clearly segregated.

Even more importantly, He was pointing out to Martha how much it matters to have our priorities straight. It's not that cooking, cleaning, and caring aren't important. Those things our vital: Communities couldn't function without women—and men—who do those jobs. But when we make them an end in themselves, forgetting the bigger picture, we feel resentful and bitter, as Martha did.

Have you ever heard yourself muttering, "Why do I have to do all the work around here? How come no one appreciates everything I do? I'm carrying this whole operation, and nobody even notices or cares!"

When we start to feel that kind of resentment, it's a good indication that we've come down with the Martha Syndrome. We've forgotten the big picture and started seeing our daily tasks as ends in themselves rather than as means to an end—loving and serving God and others.

The big picture is that God loves us and wants us to be united with Him—to be close to Him and learn from Him as Mary did when she sat at Jesus' feet. Our response to His love will be to share that love with others by serving them, whether our service takes place in the kitchen, in the classroom, in the operating room, or in the boardroom.

If we focus on the work itself and make that central, as Martha did, then we'll always be disappointed. Other people will never thank us enough, love us enough, appreciate us enough. Like Martha, we'll find ourselves locked away from the crowd, hard at work in the kitchen muttering, "Nobody appreciates me! Why aren't they in here helping out?"

"Why do I have to do all the work around here? How come no one appreciates everything I do?"

But if we put Jesus and our relationship with Him at the center of everything we do, then, like Mary, we'll have chosen the better part. It's not that we won't still have work to do. The dishes still need to be cleaned, the meal cooked, the children clothed and put to bed, the accounts tallied, the work done. Maybe after Jesus' rebuke to Martha, Mary got up and came into the kitchen to help. Maybe Jesus Himself—who loved transcending society's boundaries and surprising people—came in Himself and helped Martha get supper on the table. We don't know. The story doesn't tell us, because that's not the point.

The point is our focus. The point is our priorities.

One of my friends who is a far better housekeeper than I am has a little plaque on her wall that says "Martha doesn't live here!" The plaque refers, of course, not to the biblical Martha but to Martha Stewart, queen of gracious housekeeping, whose TV show and magazine set an impossibly high standard for homemakers.

I've often joked that there's no need for me to get a plaque like that—one glance around my casual home will assure people that Martha Stewart has never been anywhere near this place!

But maybe I'll get a "Martha doesn't live here" plaque to remind myself of Martha of Bethany, Jesus' friend and host. Even though I'm far from a compulsive housekeeper, I'm as likely as any woman to get caught up in my own priorities and my own efforts and to resent it when others don't pitch in to help, don't appreciate me enough. Maybe you have that tendency too.

Even the most worthy of tasks—such as cooking a meal for Jesus Himself—can be an opportunity for self-pity if we focus on our work rather than our relationship with the One we're serving. But the same task can be an opportunity to grow spiritually if we shift our focus to loving Jesus and learning from Him

Mary
MAGDALENE

What is a woman's word worth?
In God's eyes, more than you might think . . .

I'm telling you, it's true!"

"I'm sorry, but I just don't believe it."

"Are you doubting my word?"

It feels terrible to have someone doubt you when you're telling the absolute truth. Imagine standing in court before judge and jury with a hostile attorney cross-examining you. You do your best to tell the truth as you know it, but every word that comes out of your mouth is questioned and undermined. Your testimony seems to be worth little or nothing.

Yet you do, at least, have the right to stand in court and tell your side of the story. In the ancient Greek and Roman world, you and I wouldn't have had that privilege. Women were not allowed to act as witnesses in court. A woman could not even witness the signing of a will. Roman law stated that because of women's natural weakness and their ignorance of legal matters, no woman could speak in court; she had to be represented by a man.

In the world of the New Testament, a woman's testimony was truly worth nothing. In the chilly pre-dawn light of a Sunday morning, a woman comes to visit a tomb. She is bent with grief. The body placed there is not that of her husband, her father, or her brother, but He is the most important person in her universe. He is her Lord and Master. He delivered her from terrible bondage, and she publicly identified herself as His follower, leaving behind her known life and her family to follow Him. Now He is dead, executed as a criminal, and she comes to weep at His grave.

Her name is Mary, from Magdala. Before Jesus' death her name is mentioned only once in the Gospels. Luke 8 gives us a brief mention of Jesus' women followers. In that male-centered society they were far less well known than the 12 male disciples, but Luke tells us:

"The Twelve were with him, and also some women who had been cured of evil spirits and diseases: Mary (called Magdalene) from whom seven demons had come out; Joanna the wife of Cuza, the manager of Herod's household; Susanna; and many others. These women were helping to support them out of their own means" (verses 1-3).

This is Mary Magdalene's seven-word biography: "from whom seven demons had come out." Jesus was famous for His ability to heal and to cast out demons, and Mary had benefited from His power, whether on a single occasion, or on seven separate occasions, the Bible doesn't indicate. Nor do we know anything about her life before Jesus healed her. Christian traditions have often associated Mary Magdalene with the woman taken in adultery (John 8) and the sinful woman who washed Jesus' feet with her hair (Luke 7). Though the Bible itself doesn't identify these as being the same woman, it's certainly possible that demon possession might have led Mary to live an immoral life.

A demon-possessed woman. A sinner. If a woman's legal status in that society was low, Mary's was rock-bottom. Even after she became one of Jesus' followers, few people probably would have given much weight to her words.

Yet once the scene shifts to the events of Good Friday and the Resurrection morning, Mary's name appears everywhere in the Gospel accounts. Each of the Gospel writers notes that Mary Magdalene, along with Jesus' mother Mary and some other women, was present at the cross, at Jesus' burial, and on the morning of His resurrection. Most of Jesus' male followers disappeared, no doubt fearing that they, too, would be targets if they remained at their Leader's side. The women stayed. Though the resurrection stories differ in many details, Mary Magdalene's presence is noted in every account. During Jesus' life she is a shadowy figure watching from the sidelines. After His death she moves to center stage.

Mary's story is told in detail in John 20, where we see her alone at Jesus' tomb. On first finding the tomb empty, she calls two of the male disciples, Peter and John. They see the empty tomb and go away again, not knowing what to think. But Mary stays, weeping, and sees a Man whom she first thinks is the gardener. When He speaks her name, she recognizes Jesus.

"She turned toward him and cried out in Aramaic, 'Rabboni!' (which means Teacher). Jesus said, 'Do not hold on to me, for I have not yet returned to the Father. Go instead to my brothers and tell them, "I am returning to my Father and your Father, to my God and your God."' Mary Magdalene went to the disciples with the news: 'I have seen the Lord!' And she told them that he had said these things to her." (John 20: 16-18).

In a society in which a woman could not give testimony in court or witness a legal document, Jesus chose a woman—a woman of questionable reputation—to carry the greatest and most unbelievable news of all time to His followers. Traditionally, Mary Magdalene has been known as the Apostle to the Apostles because of her vital role as the first witness to Jesus' resurrection.

Ignore the world's judgment and accept His. He has a message for you to carry and a part for you to play.

Has anyone ever made you feel as though you were without value, as though you had no credibility? Have you been told that your words, your opinions, your testimony doesn't count—because you're a woman, because you're a sinner, because your weaknesses have been put on public display for all to see? Mary Magdalene would know just how you feel.

If she could speak to us across the centuries, what would Mary say? I think she'd say, "Have courage! Don't accept the discount labels other people put on you. Instead, measure yourself according to Jesus' value system. When other people told me I was worthless, Jesus saw value in me. When others said my word meant nothing, that my testimony had no legal weight, Jesus chose me to bear witness to His resurrection. He selected me—a woman, a sinner, an outcast—to be the first of His messengers."

Jesus can do the same for you and me. Ignore the world's judgment and accept His. He has a message for you to carry and a part for you to play. In Jesus' eyes, a woman's word is valuable enough to carry the Good News to all the world.

DORCAS

Ever feel burned out—like you have nothing left to give?
New life and new energy are possible. Just ask a woman named Dorcas.

"IN JOPPA THERE WAS A DISCIPLE NAMED . . . DORCAS,
WHO WAS ALWAYS DOING GOOD AND HELPING THE POOR" (ACTS 9:36).

Always doing good. That simple three-word motto could be used as an advertising slogan for many women. Do you ever feel like you're always doing good? Always fixing a meal, or cleaning a house, or volunteering on a committee, or listening to a friend, or washing or organizing or scrubbing or . . .?

There are many ways to be a do-gooder. Most of us have filled at least one of these roles.

There's Superwoman, who can balance housekeeping, motherhood, and a busy career without batting a perfectly made-up eyelash. She's juggling so many tasks in the air you wonder what will happen when they all come crashing down.

There's the Selfless Saint, who has given up her life in the service of another—perhaps an ailing parent, a disabled child, a dysfunctional husband, a demanding job. She seems to have no life of her own, no time to care for her own needs, no hobbies or interests of her own. When you ask how she's doing she smiles a sad little smile and says, "Oh, I mustn't complain."

And let's not forget the Busy Body . . . often a stay-at-home homemaker or a retired woman who pours her hours and energy into serving the church, running the food bank, helping the less fortunate. She can be a little bossy and officious at times, but nobody has the heart to tell her that because everyone relies so much on the work she does.

Of those three types of do-gooders—and there are many others—the woman described in Acts 9 seems to have been most like the Busy Body. She seems to have been best known for her efforts in sewing clothes for the poor, but she was probably active in helping people in many other areas too.

And what's wrong with that? Isn't that exactly the kind of work God has called Christian women to do? The Bible says of Jesus that He "went around doing good" (Acts 10:38). How honored Dorcas would have been if she'd known that almost the exact same words were used to describe her as were used to describe Jesus.

But Dorcas faced a problem. Unlike Jesus, and like all of us, she was only human. Her resources weren't limitless. All too often when we dedicate ourselves to doing good, we hit a wall that forces us to recognize our own limitations. Whether it's illness, injury, exhaustion, or the common condition called burnout, we discover that we can't keep going endlessly.

Dorcas burned out in the most conclusive way possible. She died.

We don't know how she died, or of what. The Bible simply records that "she became sick and died" (Acts 9:37). It's tempting to speculate that since Dorcas was constantly visiting the homes of the sick and poor, she may have picked up an infection in some germ-ridden, filthy hovel. Perhaps, worn out from too much work and too little rest, her immune system simply couldn't fight back. We don't know for sure, but it's entirely possible that Dorcas simply worked herself to death.

Events took a dramatic turn when the Christians in Joppa, who knew and loved Dorcas for her generous spirit, sent a message to the apostle Peter, who was visiting a nearby town. Peter – the same Peter who had been one of Jesus' three closest disciples— was well-known as a Spirit-filled preacher who had the same amazing ability to heal that Jesus, had displayed while on earth. Jesus had raised the dead. The Christians in Joppa wondered: Could Peter do the same?

Peter was willing to let God use him in this amazing way. He went straight to Dorcas's home where he was greeted by a group of poor widows who thrust into his hands robes and tunics Dorcas had sewed for them. It's as if they were saying, "Look, Peter! See what a good woman Dorcas was? She deserves to live!"

Sending them all out of the room, Peter fell to his knees and prayed. Then, confident God would answer his prayer, he commanded Dorcas to get up. The Bible tells us that, "She opened her eyes, and seeing Peter she sat up. He took her by the hand and helped her to her feet. Then he called the believers and the widows and presented her to them alive" (Acts 9:40, 41).

Wow! What a breathtaking demonstration of God's power in those exciting days right after Jesus' resurrection, when the early church was filled with God's Spirit. But what relevance does it have for us today, when such dramatic miracles rarely, if ever, occur?

While neither you nor I may ever see a person raised from the dead until Jesus' return, we can be privileged to witness—and to experience—spiritual resurrection. The most dramatic kind of "resurrection" occurs when a sinner gives her life to God and receives forgiveness and a fresh start. But I believe God can work many other miracles of resurrection in our lives. He can give new life to dying relationships, trampled hopes, expired dreams . . . and to burned-out do-gooders.

When Dorcas lay down on her bed and the last breath escaped from her body, she was no longer useful. She was no longer a strong, able woman who could fix any problem and rise to any challenge. In dying, Dorcas demonstrated in the most dramatic way possible her human weakness. She had no power left, either to help anyone else or to save herself. Nothing could save her but the power of God.

We modern Superwomen need to recognize, when we teeter on the edge of burnout, that we're not all-powerful. While we can be God's agents in bringing His love to a broken world, we're not God. We're only human. We have limitations. We need eight hours of sleep nightly and a Sabbath day off once a week. We need God's power—His resurrection power—flowing through us.

When the effort of being good, of doing good, of serving and helping and loving and caring, seems so great that you're ready to burn out . . . stop. Lie down, both physically and spiritually. Rest in the knowledge that God is in control—and you're not. And allow a space in your life for His healing, His resurrection power, to reach you.

An old saying tells us, "You can't draw water from a dry well." But many of us twenty-first-century Dorcases have become so efficient at pumping out blessings to others that we've allowed ourselves to dry out. We need spiritual restoration, renewal, and resurrection. We need God's healing power in our own lives before we can continue to be any use to those around us.

If you're on the verge of burnout, don't keep working till you drop. Rather, drop to your knees (or into a comfortable chair) right now and ask God to refill and restore you. Taking time to renew your spirit isn't selfish—it's essential.

LYDIA

Do you feel like you don't quite fit in?
Like you're always the one left on the outside of every circle?
Lydia could have told you about the One who invites you in to His inner circle...

On a Sabbath morning, on a riverbank outside the city walls of Philippi, a small group of women gathered for worship. One of them—perhaps their leader—was a woman named Lydia whom the Bible tells us "worshipped God" and was a "seller of purple" (Acts 16:14, NKJV).

Those few phrases give us a glimpse into Lydia's life. As a seller of purple dye, she was a dealer in one of the most valuable luxury commodities in the ancient world. Purple dye was imported from Tyre, where it was made from sea snails through a difficult and expensive process. Only the most wealthy and important people could afford to wear Tyrean purple, as it was called, so Lydia's customers must have been among the leading citizens of Philippi. She herself would have been a wealthy and well-respected member of the merchant class.

Yet her name appears in the Bible alone, suggesting that she was unmarried, for a married woman would have been known as "Lydia, wife of ...." As a merchant and businesswoman in her own right, she was most likely a widow, perhaps carrying on the family business after her husband's death. Such a role for a prosperous widow was not unheard-of, but Lydia would have been a woman in a man's world, competing against men in the marketplace. She was also an outsider to Philippi, coming originally from the city of Thyatria in Asia. While she was apparently very successful at her work, Lydia most likely remained an outsider in the men's world of business and in the society of a Roman town.

When she came to worship God, Lydia was also an outsider—on two counts. The little group with which she worshipped met outside the city walls on the Jewish Sabbath. They were worshipping the God of Israel, and it's possible they had to meet outside the city because their worship was not considered acceptable within the Roman city. Jews were outsiders, often excluded and scorned because they refused to worship the Greek and Roman gods.

There is one place where you will always be accepted. One Person Who will always consider you part of His inner circle. With Jesus, there is acceptance and belonging.

But Lydia probably wasn't a Jew. The Bible describes her as a woman who "worshipped God." The Greek word used in this verse is one that was used for pagans who worshipped the God of Israel and learned from the Jewish Scriptures, but who had not become full converts to Judaism. Lydia, apparently a well-off and successful pagan woman, was drawn to the God she found in the Jewish Scriptures. Yet, for whatever reason, she did not choose to take the final step of converting to Judaism. She worshipped that God, but she worshipped as an outsider among outsiders. Nowhere—not in the marketplace, not in the pagan temples of Philippi, not even among the Jews—was she completely at home.

Maybe you've felt like Lydia. Like her, you may look successful on the outside, but inside there's a yearning to fit in, to belong, that you feel will never quite be satisfied. Perhaps you've moved to a new community and you feel you'll always be an outsider there. Maybe your in-laws have a way of making you feel like an interloper who'll never be part of the family. Perhaps even in church you find yourself thinking, I'll never fit in with these people! There's nobody here who understands me.

We human beings have a built-in desire to belong. It's one of our most basic needs. We want to feel part of a family, part of a community, part of a network of people who understand and love and care about us. It's what we all need. But all too often it's not what we get.

Given Lydia's "outsider" status, we might expect to see her on the fringes of the group, hanging back, afraid to speak her mind. But she's the one person mentioned by name in the Acts 16 account of the founding of the Philippi church. She was the first person baptized as a Christian in Macedonia.

Not only did she accept the Christian message, this wealthy woman made herself a patron to Paul and the rest of the missionary party by offering them her home to live in. Acts 16:15 records Lydia's invitation: "'If you consider me a believer in the Lord,' she said, 'come and stay at my house.'"

All her life, whether through circumstance or choice, Lydia remained on the outer fringes of every group. She carved out a successful life for herself out there on the margins, but she never truly belonged. But when Paul came preaching the word of Jesus, Lydia threw herself wholeheartedly into the center of the new Christian movement. This woman who had held back from converting to Judaism had no hesitation at all about being baptized as soon as she heard the message of Jesus.

Perhaps when Lydia heard the stories of Jesus, she recognized Someone Who could fully accept her. Jesus' was famous, sometimes even infamous, for accepting people. He made room in the circles around Him for thieves and prostitutes, wealthy tax collectors and Pharisees, women and children, and even Gentiles like Lydia. He drew a circle that was wide enough to include everybody—and some were shocked and scandalized at how inclusive He was.

After Jesus' death and resurrection, His followers carried on the same openness. Greek and Roman observers shook their heads in dismay at these Christians who allowed everyone—Jew and Gentile, male and female, slave and free—to worship together and even take leadership roles. The carefully drawn boundaries that kept everyone in his or her place were shattered by the open arms of Jesus.

Maybe that was what Lydia responded to. She never met Jesus, yet when Paul and the others talked about Him, she heard in those stories a message of welcome and acceptance. A message that told her she would never need to be an outsider again. A message that said Jesus loved her as much as He loved anyone. Loved her for who she was—Lydia, the purple dye merchant of Philippi. His arms reached out and took her in.

Those arms are reaching out for you. If you feel excluded, marginalized, alone—remember there is one place where you will always be accepted. One Person Who will always consider you part of His inner circle. With Jesus, there is acceptance and belonging. And He invites you, like Lydia, to dive in to the center of His love.

EUODIA & SYNTYCHE

Have you ever had a terrible argument that wouldn't stop?
Maybe it was with a co-worker, a fellow church member, a relative.
Most of us have had that experience . . . including two early Christians
whose names are remembered only because of their argument.

"Can you believe what she said about me?"

"I was devastated by what she did!"

"Those were the most hurtful words I've ever heard—and she's supposed to be a Christian!"

We've all been there. A painful, devastating argument. The "enemy" might be your co-worker, the woman in the next pew at church, your mother-in-law, sister, or former best friend. Somehow you end up on opposite sides of an issue or there's a misunderstanding. Words are said that can't be taken back or forgotten. Apologies are avoided—or ignored. Suddenly a vast chasm of wounded feelings and insults stands between you, and you see no way to leap over the gap.

It seems especially devastating when this kind of a quarrel breaks out between women who are supposed to be sisters in Christ, sharing the bond of Christian love and unity. But it happens all too often. Something as small as a misplaced dish at a church potluck can set off a chain reaction of accusations and pointed fingers. Before we know it, gossip and slander have taken the wheel and tossed Christian sisterhood out the window.

It's not a modern problem. We know for certain that a similar situation occurred in one of the very earliest Christian churches. Just a few decades after Jesus' death, two well-meaning church ladies were bad-mouthing each other all over the city of Philippi. Their quarrel grew so serious that it affected the whole church—and drew the attention of the great missionary, evangelist and letter-writer Paul himself.

"I plead with Euodia and I plead with Syntyche to agree with each other in the Lord. Yes, and I ask you, loyal yokefellow, help these women who have contended at my side in the cause of the gospel" (Philippians 4:2, 3).

Those words in the fourth chapter of the letter to the Philippians are the only time Euodia's and Syntyche's names are mentioned in the Bible. We know absolutely nothing about these women other than what is mentioned in this verse. No background, no history—and nothing about the quarrel that divided them. We don't know whether it started over a huge doctrinal issue or a tiny personal misunderstanding. The fact is, the cause doesn't matter. By the time a situation has gotten this far out of hand, all that matters is the damage that's being done— and finding a way to stop it.

What we do know from this verse is that Euodia and Syntyche were both Christians— and both prominent members of the Philippian church. In fact, they were probably both leaders, since Paul says that they "contended at his side in the cause of the gospel." These women were involved in ministry, in leadership positions, pillars in the church and community. The only problem was that they couldn't get along.

We all know how these situations work. By the time it got this big, the quarrel would no longer have involved just Euodia and Syntyche. Euodia's husband probably wouldn't speak to Syntyche's brother when they met in the marketplace. Their children were no longer allowed to play together. Church members lined up to take one side or the other. What began as a private quarrel ended up dividing a church. It happened in Philippi; it still happens today.

Notice that Paul doesn't take sides. He doesn't say, "Euodia, you know Syntyche's right, so stop opposing her. Apologize!" He directs his advice to both women: they both know there's a problem and they have both contributed to it. They both have a role to play in making it right. He's not concerned with assigning blame or going back to the roots of the problem. He wants both women to take equal responsibility.

But he also gives both women credit. They are hard workers. They have done their part in helping to spread the gospel. They are committed Christian women, and that's why their quarrel is such a tragedy.

If you've been involved in an ongoing, heart-wrenching disagreement, you may begin to feel that you're a bad person and a bad Christian because of that. Conflict can sap your self-esteem and have you believing the negative things others have said about you.

Take a lesson from Paul as he addresses Euodia and Syntyche. Acknowledge that you're a good person caught in a bad situation. Chances are, even if you can't see at the moment, your opponent is a good person too. You both have your strengths, your gifts, your

They were both working toward the same goal—the kingdom of God. But their private quarrel had grown so huge that it stood in the way of that goal.

abilities. Neither of you are evil people because you've become involved in a controversy.

You're not a bad person because of this conflict. But you're not a helpless victim either. Like Euodia and Syntyche, you have the ability to change things. It may take two people to start a quarrel, but it only takes one to say, "It's time to stop." Pride often holds us back from taking that first step. We don't want to be the one who gives in, the one who "caves," the one who takes that first slice of humble pie.

But that's the Christian way. That's Jesus' way. That's the way Paul appealed to Euodia and Syntyche to try. He begged them to put aside hurt pride, legitimate grievances, insults and offenses, and look at the bigger picture. They were both working toward the same goal—the kingdom of God. But their private quarrel had grown so huge that it stood in the way of that goal. It was time for someone to take the first step to reconciliation.

Just as Euodia and Syntyche are never mentioned in the Bible before this incident, they're never mentioned afterward, either. We don't know the sequel to the story. Was the quarrel ever resolved?

In one family I know, a bitter 10-year family quarrel ended when one woman picked up the phone, called another, and said, "This has gone on long enough. Will you and your family come to dinner with us this Sabbath?"

I'd like to imagine Euodia or Syntyche doing the same thing. There was no phone service in first-century Philippi, of course, but maybe one woman or the other, after reading Paul's letter, strapped on her sandals and walked down the dusty road to the other woman's house. Her heart must have pounded with fear, but maybe she knocked on the door and said, "This has gone on long enough. Let's ask the Lord to forgive us both, and help us start again. Can you come to dinner?"